B&T
$7.95
22 Feb'79

WHAT WAS FREEDOM'S PRICE?

What Was Freedom's Price?

Essays by

WILLIE LEE ROSE

JOEL WILLIAMSON

RICHARD SUTCH & ROGER RANSOM

GEORGE M. FREDRICKSON

C. VANN WOODWARD

Edited by
DAVID G. SANSING

UNIVERSITY PRESS OF MISSISSIPPI

JACKSON 1978

Copyright © 1978 by the
University Press of Mississippi
Manufactured in the United States of America

This volume is sponsored by the
University of Mississippi

Library of Congress Cataloging in Publication Data
Main entry under title:

What was freedom's price.

   CONTENTS: Rose, W. L. Jubilee & beyond.—
Williamson, J. W. E. B. Du Bois as a Hegelian.—
Sutch, R. & Ransom, R. Sharecropping. [etc.]
   1. Southern States—History—1865- —Addresses,
essays, lectures.   2. Reconstruction—Addresses,
essays, lectures.   3. Afro-Americans—Southern States
—History—Addresses, essays, lectures.   4. Southern
States—Social conditions—Addresses, essays, lectures.
5. Southern States—Economic conditions—Addresses,
essays, lectures.   I. Rose, Willie Lee Nichols,
1927-   II. Sansing, David G.
F215.W5   975'.004'96073   78-3736
ISBN 0–87805–046–9
ISBN 0–87805–048–5 pbk.

This volume is dedicated to
JAMES WESLEY SILVER,
FORMER PRESIDENT OF THE
SOUTHERN HISTORICAL ASSOCIATION
SCHOLAR, TEACHER, & COLLEAGUE

Contents

Introduction

In the day of jubilee a refrain echoed and richocheted throughout the American South—"Praise God! We're Free! Free at last!"
And the nation breathed a collective sigh of relief, "It's over.
. . . We are done with slavery." There was some impressive evidence in the fall of 1865 that even southerners were relieved to
be done with slavery and expressions of loyalty from what appeared to be a new southern leadership convinced President
Andrew Johnson that southerners could and should be trusted
with their own reconstruction. Southerners would, he insisted, be
fair and just with the freedmen as they legislated economic
recovery and racial readjustment. But, the enactment of the black
codes by southern legislatures which severely restricted the
social, economic, and political activity of southern blacks com-
promised Johnson's credibility and undermined Presidential Reconstruction. Radical Republicans, who advocated a more puni
tive Reconstruction than did the President, made the black codes
a major political issue in the fall elections of 1866. Republican
congressional candidates also emphasized the southern President's role in the rejection of the Fourteenth Amendment, his
truculent attitude toward Congress, and his determination to
allow the South as much latitude as possible in their own Reconstruction. Following that election, which resulted in a Radical-
controlled and veto-proof Congress, the President lost control of
Reconstruction policy and Congress enacted a series of laws

which brought sweeping changes to the southern economy and social structure.

This legislation was the culmination of what some southern leaders had feared most and had vainly attempted to forestall by warning President Johnson to proceed slowly and cautiously in assessing the signs of returning loyalty and acquiescence among the southern people. John F. H. Claiborne of Mississippi, for example, had written to the President as early as May, 1865, warning Johnson that southerners were not prepared for the pyschological consequences of military defeat or the social and economic consequences of emancipation. Claiborne recommended the continuation of military government for at least another year. It would take time, he argued, for southerners to realize what had happened to them and to recoup and to readjust.

"There is," according to Arnold J. Toynbee, "a thing called history, but history is something unpleasant that happens to other people . . . if I had been a small boy in . . . the southern part of the United States, I should not have felt the same; I should have known from my parents that history had happened to my people in my part of the world." History happened to southerners during the Civil War and they were dazzled by the dimensions and blinding speed of that cataclysm. Perhaps few documents reveal the repercussions of that cataclysm in such intimate, human terms as does the following letter.

> House of Representatives
> Jackson, Mississippi
> March 26, 1870

To His Excellency Governor James L. Alcorn:

Governor, I was a slave of Col. W. G. Henderson. Boys together as we were, he is the center of the tenderest associations of my life. Arrived at manhood's estate, I was still intimately connected with him. . . . When he was wounded at Upperville, . . . he languished in the valley of Virginia . . . until it was my privilege to take him away, secretly, through the lines to his own people.

My friend and loving master is a candidate for . . . Circuit Judge . . . and a good republican.

Now, Governor, I, by the mysterious providence of God, am a member of the Legislature . . . and I now place . . . my earnest prayer that you appoint to the Judgeship of the First District the playmate of my boyhood, the companion of my manhood, the generous friend of my whole life—my former master, Col. Henderson.

/s/ Ambrose Henderson

Yet, while Henderson was writing this letter and while four million other freedmen were revelling in their freedom, forces were already in motion that would restrain and constrain and all but abort that freedom. Economic complexities, social intricacies, political expediences, racial prejudices, and other idiosyncrasies of the southern character—each powerful forces in themselves—combined to produce a postwar society in which the black man occupied a status somewhere between slavery and full citizenship. But all blacks were not lodged at a given point on the scale between slavery and citizenship. The gap was great and blacks were clustered at various levels with some enjoying a greater measure of freedom than others.

The structure was, however, "bottom heavy" and most blacks lived closer to slavery than they did to full citizenship. Sharecropping replaced slavery as a labor system but was as fundamentally characteristic of southern agriculture after the war as slavery was before. With its relentless demands on the land, sharecropping eroded and gullied the southern landscape. It also eroded and gullied the southern Negro's control over his personal and collective destiny. Blacks were free under the law, but they could not leave "Mussa Gilmo's place, 'causen he wud'n let'm."

For most black sharecroppers a residue of slavery lingered in their lives. Thousands of southern blacks, perhaps hundreds of thousands, lived in the same or similar shacks they had occupied as slaves, ate the same food, wore the same clothes, plowed the same fields, walked the same paths, drank from the same wells. The cotton and the corn were the same; they needed rain at certain times and sunshine at other times and they never seemed to get enough of either at the right time. The sharecropper continued to receive his rations. Many, perhaps most, were not paid for their work and did not pay for their keep. Most, practically all, never broke even and were carried on the books from year to year and year after year. When land was sold the books went with the land and the sharecroppers went with the books.

What was freedom like to these blacks and to other blacks suspended—or trapped—in that never-never land between slavery and citizenship? Did emancipation produce a social revolution for blacks? Were there viable alternatives to a dual society with each race segregated from the other? Was sharecropping a racial mechanism or a market response to southern economic conditions? How did other former slave societies adjust to and cope with emancipation? Did or could America have profited from their experiences? The five original essays presented in this volume examine these questions and probe the results of economic, social, and racial readjustment in the post Civil War South.

These papers were presented at the second annual Chancellor's Symposium on Southern History held at the University of Mississippi September 22–24, 1976. Appearing in the order in which they were presented at the symposium, these essays represent the latest research of six major scholars in the postwar period. Additionally, a recognized scholar also presided at each session of the conference and offered a brief commentary on the paper before opening the floor for general discussion. The department of history would like to express its appreciation to those scholars who include James McPherson, Herbert Gutman, Harold D. Woodman, Mary Berry, and Louis Harlan. We also wish to thank Chancellor Porter L. Fortune, Jr. for his continued interest in and support of the symposium, Dr. Arthur H. DeRosier, former Vice-Chancellor for Academic Affairs, Dr. Joe Sam, Dean of the Graduate School, Dr. Gerald Walton, Dean of the College of Liberal Arts, Mrs. George W. Howell, departmental secretary, and the Division of Continuing Education for their assistance in coordinating the various arrangements for the symposium. I would personally like to thank the members of the department of history, especially Robert J. Haws and Michael V. Namorato, for their assistance throughout the long period of planning for the symposium and the publication of these essays, and Barney McKee, director of the University Press of Mississippi, for his continued interest and assistance in the publication of the papers presented at the Chancellor's Symposium on Southern History.

David G. Sansing
University of Mississippi
Oxford, Mississippi

WHAT WAS FREEDOM'S PRICE?

Jubilee & Beyond:
What Was Freedom?

WILLIE LEE ROSE

Now no larger than a human hand on the horizon of our labors, a new question is forming for historians of the Civil War and Reconstruction. Bluntly put, it asks whether the Reconstruction constituted in any real sense a social revolution. This should not be confused with the older question that Charles Beard investigated, whether the Civil War and its aftermath brought on a victory for the industrial and commercial interests of the North over the plantation system and its interests, for one might answer that question either way and still fail to address the issue of what emancipation meant for the four million slaves released in the course of the Civil War. Legally, the changes wrought by emancipation and the war amendments were colossal: when in history have so many people been so abruptly transformed from chattel property to a constitutionally equal status; from the objects of contracts among their owners to responsible agents able to make contracts of their own and to be held to them; from the subjects of police regulation of the sort associated with the control of criminal elements in an uneasy population to free soldiers and militiamen of the Republic; from a people denied education because it was held to be dangerous for them to have it to possessors of the elective franchise?

Perhaps because our own United States history offers no swift

3

changes in status so dramatic as these, our scholars have fallen into the habit of assuming that the Civil War did indeed launch a social revolution. Allan Nevins entitled the volume of his monumental narrative history of the war that includes the Emancipation quite simply *War Becomes Revolution*. David Brion Davis has referred to the "revolutionary implications of mass emancipation," and C. Vann Woodward has written about the change that took place during the war from "a pragmatic struggle for power" to "a crusade for ideals" that embraced "revolutionary aims." I could go on and on, and I should no doubt confess that my own typewriter had a tendency once to discourse perhaps too uncritically about social revolutions.[1] Professor Woodward has had reason to change the emphasis he once placed on the Radical Republicans' commitment to the goal of equality, and many other scholars (including Jacques Voegeli, Richard Curry, Forrest G. Wood, and William McFeely) have been so thoroughly impressed by the depth of northern prejudice against blacks in the period under question, as well as so overcome by the exploitative and rigid policies of the military authorities regarding freedmen during the occupation, that they have placed the whole conception of a revolution in jeopardy.[2] Even scholars who have used the concept of revolution have always been aware of the sharp reaction following the crest of political Reconstruction. Recognizing that freedmen were shortly forced back toward agricultural peonage, driven out of politics, and reduced to second-class citizenship in the courts as well as in bars and drugstores, historians have been inclined to refer to these events as an "aborted" revolution, an "unrealized" revolution, or one that "miscarried."[3]

The sharpest recent statement of complete rejection comes from Louis Gerteis, whose book *From Contraband to Freedom: Federal Policy Toward Southern Blacks, 1861–65* (1973) directly challenges the assumption that the war and Reconstruction "brought dramatic and fundamental changes in the society and economy of the South." Professor Gerteis believes that "the details of federal labor policies and the war-time failure of Radical reforms indicate that emancipation did not involve specific changes in the status of the former slaves or the conditions under which they labored." In short, no revolution occurred, or was even contemplated, because the government (and northern voters behind the government, presumably) did not want one.[4] In response it is easily arguable that intentions do not foretell specific results, especially in revolutionary situations, even though weak motivation may sometimes explain failure. Gerteis—in setting forth the grim details of the army's dealings with refugee blacks, its employment of freedmen as contract labor on the plantations, sometimes under the supervision of the very men who had recently been their owners, the rigorous physical discipline of these laborers—has done a real service, and he clearly shows that for the time being, at any rate, the army had no intention of interfering with the then de facto status of the freedmen as agricultural peasants.

This is a good lesson for readers who may yet be under some illusion about the crusading role of the United States Army. But a demonstration that there was no constructive plan during the war aimed at a "sociology of freedom" does not rule out the possibility that the political goals of Reconstruction, involving the establishment of a "loyal"—and yes—a Republican electorate in the southern states, an electorate that had necessarily to rest largely on black votes, might have opened the door (even if inadvertently) to more far-reaching changes. So narrow a view of what occurred during Reconstruction, one based so exclusively on flawed motives of the emancipators and on lasting results, also has the effect of wrongly outflanking the significance of emancipation for the freedmen themselves; it ignores their perceptions of the great event, their hopes and fears for the future. Does their immediate response, decampment from the plantations in the wake of the armies, their celebration of the day of jubilee, count for nothing? Was theirs a foolish response to a counterfactual event? This is clearly one of those questions that may be answered and defended in both the negative and positive.

Marxist historians require that a social revolution bring about a durable shift of power from one identifiable social class to another. By this standard the Emancipation Proclamation could hardly qualify, but then few revolutions have abruptly brought such sharp transformations in human affairs. Fortunately most historians implicitly accept a working definition somewhere short of that, and they regard an event that brings important changes in the way people live, work, and make their power felt as being revolutionary. At this point, the question of time immediately clamors for attention when a historian considers the American Civil War and Reconstruction. What is a reasonable period for the registration of these important changes?

From the perspective of a century, the legal gains and the fundamental constitutional amendments of the postwar era do seem revolutionary, for their potentialities have now been exploited to a remarkable degree. Yet one does not applaud heartily for the award of vouchers redeemable only in the fourth generation. Surely a century of waiting is too long for even the most optimistic; surely something short of that must serve. Could the emancipation have been regarded as "revolutionary" in 1863? In 1867? In 1877? In 1883? In 1896, still only one long generation from the Reconstruction upheaval? By 1896 the reaction had crystallized in the Supreme Court's endorsement of the separate-but-equal doctrine in *Plessy* v. *Ferguson,* and the nation, the whole country, had come to so low a point in race relations that it has been properly termed the "nadir," with violence rampant, lynchings increasingly focused on blacks exclusively and usually unpunished, and blacks on the plantations reduced to peonage as sharecroppers unable to free themselves from debt.[5] Whatever implications the year 1896 carried were surely counterrevolutionary or even less significant than that, if we can agree that the reaction against the acts of emancipation and Reconstruction was in full course well ahead of *Plessy* v. *Ferguson*. Even by 1883 most of the legal guarantees secured by the three war amendments and the civil rights acts of 1866 and 1875 had been vitiated, if not obliterated.

If after 1896 the southern states made systematic assaults on black voting rights, the ground had been prepared well in advance by earlier decisions distinguishing between state and national citizenship and placing only the rights of national citizenship under federal protection.[6] In 1883 the decision of the Supreme Court in the civil rights cases merely endorsed current practice in large parts of the country. If no later year will serve, then 1877 certainly cannot be pressed into service, for in that year, in the famous arrangement Professor Woodward and others have so well described, the Republican party seated its candidate in the office of the president, in return for certain economic considerations to the South as a region and for the social consideration of leaving the "Southern Question" to the white South to resolve.[7] The losers were Samuel J. Tilden, who had probably won the election by fair means or foul, and the southern blacks, who were left to such hope as they might extract from assurances that they would not be deprived of the legal gains they had made in the Reconstruction acts. If these assurances were disregarded and forgotten, there were probably very few persons, white or black, North or South, who were honestly surprised.

Steady pressure on the legal position of freedmen was matched by declining economic opportunities. The comparatively fluid position of blacks in the first five or ten years of their freedom was steadily hardening into the new form of economic subordination destined to replace slavery—the system based on tenantry, sharecropping, and the crop-lien system. Carried out within a framework of state legislation forbidding enticement of labor off the plantation, enforcing contracts, and punishing vagrancy, the new system had much the look of slavery; it is tempting to equate the black way of life in the New South with that in the Old South, with the interesting difference that many blacks, most perhaps, had now less protection from the violence of society at large than they had once had as valuable property. As William Cohen has recently written, the new forms of economic servitude were "involuntary," as were the old, and, precisely because they were established in laws that omitted mention of race, they reflected a mutual understanding and community of interest among all whites to see that they were applied *particularly* to black laborers.[8] These laws, devised first in the black codes created just after the war, when the white South was given a free hand under the Johnson administration, were erased from the books after the Radical triumph of late 1866 and the establishment of the Republican state governments; they were, however, restored and developed for practical service after these Republican governments were overthrown and lasted well into the twentieth century as the legal basis of agricultural peonage. They definitely discourage the search for any revolutionary social tendencies owing to emancipation developing after the 1870s and before our own times.

There remains then only to consider for evidence of social revolution the high period of Reconstruction endeavor, from emancipation during the Civil War to the Reconstruction acts of 1867 and the establishment of Republican state governments in the South. Much that was achieved was subsequently eroded, but how much was achieved? Enough to constitute a social revolution as well as a legal and political one?

Blacks seemed to think so. Lack of personal mobility is surely the most overt condition of slavery, and this constraint was the first that blacks put to the test. Understanding the meaning of the war to their own prospects ahead of most northern voters, blacks responded to the presence of federal soldiers in all sectors by massive flight from the plantations, well before the Emancipation Proclamation and with such enthusiasm that dealing with fugitive slaves became the entering wedge that led eventually to emancipation as a federal war policy. The question for the North was not necessarily humanitarian, certainly at the beginning, but quite simply put it asked why northern generals should send slaves back to their plantations to work for the general health of the Confederacy. Although idealists might have better reasons by modern standards, even the most hidebound racist of the 1860s would want to know that much. For their part, blacks who deserted the plantations were hastening the day of jubilee by creating such confusion that the old world could never be reconstructed in the same way. Their individual goals were various, sometimes to reunite with family and friends, but there was often no more specific object than trying out the novel right to come and go at will. This is a characteristic feature of social upheavals, as observers of others revolutions have confirmed.

If blacks showed their faith in the coming revolution by flight, the slave owners also reacted as though in fear of insurrections and reprisals, threatening to "make examples" of more energetic and demonstrative freedmen, by imploring the protection of federal soldiers in areas where blacks were in arms, either as federal troops or later on in the state militias under the Radical state governments.[9] While blacks snatched their liberty when and where they could and announced their intention to take it seriously by immediately placing land of their own as their first priority and by snatching grammar lessons from anybody who would teach them, whites strove to retain as much of the old life as they were able, through opposing blacks' access to land, making life as hard as possible for the intruders who came to teach them, and then by organizing paramilitary groups like the Ku Klux Klan to frighten them into submission. The touching obverse of these aspects of white fear and hostility was the pathetic gratitude of former masters and mistresses to those of

their former "servants" who spurned the temptations of freedom
—or seemed to do so—and affirmed their faith in the old order
by despising yankees and the new dispensation.[10]

But these responses and counterresponses, it must be con-
fessed, do little more than register the hopes and fears of the
war and the first year of peace. As Professor Gerteis has pointed
out, most southern blacks learned of their freedom not from a
Union cavalry officer galloping up to the plantation and telling
the slaves they were free to go where they pleased, but from
their erstwhile owners, who assembled them to announce their
new status and to offer continued employment, sometimes for
pay, sometimes for nothing beyond what the plantation might
yield in food and provisions. However frayed at the edges the
Confederacy was in 1865, there were more plantations that did
not experience the passage of Union troops than *did* and more
slaves who did not run away to the Union lines than the large
minority who made the attempt.[11] In spite of white fears, there
was relatively little overt resistance among the plantation workers, most of it confined to the parishes of southern Louisiana,
where restlessness and rebellion were apparently inspired by the
proximity of black troops and promptly put down by the United
States Army.

Yet knowledge about freedmen who experienced this change
as a consequence of invading armies spread far and wide among
plantation blacks, and one aspect of this upheaval stirred the
imagination of all: some blacks had been given land. In dealing
with the massive influx of refugee slaves, federal officers were
solving their problem by putting them to work as quickly as possible. Although working as forced labor on abandoned plantations undoubtedly had small attraction for slaves in the western
sector of the fighting, circumstances were different elsewhere.
On the East Coast planters had very early in the war abandoned
their lands in large areas to the invading armies, and under the
Direct Tax Act of 1861 these plantations were confiscated by

the government and in the process of being sold again to individuals. In many instances blacks there had been offered the chance to buy land on preferred terms. Then General William Tecumseh Sherman solved the problem of the thousands of refugees who had followed him out of Georgia by settling them on the islands and estuarial property in South Carolina and Georgia. Thus the hope to obtain land of their own was most sharply boosted by that general who probably disliked blacks the most. But the Civil War abounded in ironies, and Sherman as the father of the "forty-acres-and-mule" dream is no more astonishing than that this experiment should be carried out in the part of the Confederacy that had worked hardest and longest for secession.[12] At all events the idea circulated widely in the interior and, combined with the wording of the new Freedmen's Bureau Act, which spoke of settling the freedmen on abandoned lands with such "title" as the government "could convey," raised restless expectations that were not easily put down.

Blacks resisted entering into contracts with white landowners in the year after the war, for fear they might then be unable to take advantage of the hoped-for chance to settle on land of their own. Dan T. Carter is probably quite correct in his analysis that the famous Christmas insurrection scare of 1865 was more a product of white fear than of a concerted plan among the blacks, but there was indeed extreme tension in the fall and winter of 1865, which came to very sharp focus when President Andrew Johnson began pardoning former Confederates and restoring their property. Blacks who were already working on these lands showed marked hostility to the news that they would be dispossessed when their crops were harvested. The black farmers of Sapelo Island fired on troops sent to evict them, and throughout the region committees of freedmen voiced their determination to keep their land if they could but, in any case, to avoid the alternative that looked to them most like slavery: working in gangs for pay on land owned by others.[13]

But restoration went forward inexorably, and, except for a few islands where properties had been sold to private persons under the Direct Tax Act, there was no abandoned land left for black settlement. The freedmen were made to choose between eviction and making contracts with the owners. This was no easy task, but the government succeeded in forcing the choice, and the Freedmen's Bureau took the responsibility for approving the equity of arrangements.

After 1865 the idea of providing freedmen with land withered away. It is a signal fact that only one of the states, even under Radical Republican government, made an effort to assist freedmen in purchasing land on preferred terms and that this effort was so plagued by corruption that it never served its purpose. The federal government might have undertaken to distribute public lands owned in the Confederate states and to provide for many freedmen's families, but it did not do so.[14] The collapse of the movement to lay an economic foundation under the freedmen's liberty meant that the plantation system would survive, that slavery would be replaced eventually by the crop-lien system of exploitation, and that there would be no revolution in land tenure.

Whether extensive land reform would have made a difference in the time actually required to develop the social and economic freedom that was not established in Reconstruction has already been the subject of quiet debate. In an elegant comparative essay Professor Woodward has pointed out that in all societies the process of emancipation has been followed by a period of economic exploitation and semifree status.[15] There is reason to suppose that a people like the freedmen, lacking education, political experience, and seasoned leadership and forming a numerical minority, would have lost in a struggle, however stoutly mounted, to retain their land. The success of antebellum agriculture rested to a considerable extent on the advantages of scale. Unsuitable for small farms, the great southern staples required much capital and credit to withstand the shocks of a sequence of bad years and more organization and cooperation among producers and specialization among laborers.[16] None of this could have been provided by freedmen seated on small acreages of twenty or forty acres, even over many decades, decades in which these little farms would have been under the most intense pressure. Given the specific circumstances then prevailing, it is probable that these properties would have soon been absorbed again into larger units. If, on the other hand, a federal policy had been devised to prevent the sale of these farms for a number of years and to sustain the freedmen as landowners for a lengthy period, it is easy to believe that large-scale production of cotton, sugar, and rice would have been displaced by subsistence farming, with each family raising food crops as a first priority and a few staples for a little "cash money." This is why efforts at cooperative purchase and management initially worked better for the freedmen than isolated individual purchases. These collective endeavors were always led by men who had had previous experience under slavery as farm managers or drivers. On Jefferson Davis's plantation at Davis Bend, Ben Montgomery performed this service and saw to it that the blacks on these Mississippi Delta plantations were engaged in productive labor, even while the war was still raging around them and while less fortunate freedmen in the vicinity were being worked by the U.S. Army on leased plantations, often forced to their labor with crude methods on a par with later convict-lease methods. Although the army claimed credit for the successes at Davis Bend, a close consideration of the individual case has caused James T. Currie to conclude that the early success and productivity of these freedmen owed a lot to Ben Montgomery's having kept the army and the Freedmen's Bureau *out* of Davis Bend.[17] Here and there throughout the South examples of similar efforts could be cited. To live on the old home place among family and friends, without the master and his "peculiar institution," seemed for most freedmen the happiest culmination of events, and the ablest of the farmers among them saw the economic advantages of collective effort over individual ownership of small plots. What would one do for water, woodlands, access roads, and barns for livestock, if restricted to a twenty- or forty-acre cotton field? These very questions were raised by blacks in the Sea Islands when specific plans were being laid out for dividing the plantations among the freedmen. A consequence foreseen by only a few at the time was the ultimate division and subdivision of the lands through inheritance into even smaller units until they were of negligible economic value. Edward Philbrick of Massachusetts opposed subdivision of the large plantations for this reason (among others less defensible), claiming that that was what had happened in France after the French Revolution. Philbrick was not an entirely disinterested observer, but what he said would happen did in fact happen on St. Helena Island, South Carolina, one of the very few large swatches of land that experienced the kind of revolution in landholding that the best friends of the freedmen wanted for them.[18] I do not intend here to argue that freedmen got out of Reconstruction all that they might reasonably have expected, but merely to note that the forty-acres-and-a-mule promise has been too dogmatically advanced as the great might-have-been that could have best aided freedmen to achieve economic independence.

But lack of imagination in the plans of Republican idealists was not the real reason so little was done. The real reason was that the number of persons who wanted an economic program to undergird emancipation was always very small. If the will had existed while the war was being fought, some effective program might have benefited from the wartime emotion of vengeance against the slaveholders. But the will did not exist. Emancipation came piecemeal and as a war measure; it was unpopular in a racist society that visited upon free blacks the daily indignities of segregation and second-class citizenship, but it was acceptable as a means of wounding the enemy. One has to look no farther than this to explain the cold language of the Emancipation Proclamation, which is not memorable for quote-worthy sentiments and has inspired no schoolchild to rhetorical flourishes. The document of January 1, 1863, was more a threat to slaveholders than a promise to slaves, releasing slaves only in areas the federal armies had not penetrated. Slaves themselves were enjoined against violence, and in practice Union troops suppressed insurrections on several occasions.[19]

And yet this cautiously advanced document inaugurated a chain of events that led to greater political gains than any but the most sanguine could have imagined in 1863, gains so sweeping that they could not be entirely erased in the period of reaction that followed the overthrow of the Republican state governments. Whether one calls these changes a revolution is a matter of individual semantic preference, but I do not doubt that the southern people, whites and blacks, who experienced them, thought they were involved in a revolution. Without saying so directly, the document represented a bargain with blacks that resulted in their prompt enlistment in the Union armies and consequently placed the northern people under an obligation that could not be ignored in the peace, or altogether ignored. If the right to vote, when it came, owed more to the Republican majority's need to create a new political force in the South than to idealism or guilt, it is still a little hard to see how the Fourteenth Amendment could have been forced upon the South through the military Reconstruction acts without the burst of indignation that followed the southern states' enactment of the black codes, which were understood in the North as a new form of slavery, and without the race riots in Memphis and New Orleans.[20] Protecting blacks in their freedom seems to have been the bottom line (and maybe the top as well) for most northern voters, but protecting that narrowly defined political freedom eventually appeared to require the Freedmen's Bureau, two civil rights acts, and three amendments to the Constitution, not to speak of the military Reconstruction acts.

If the war itself was the cause and the momentum of emancipation and subsequent commitments, however halfheartedly undertaken, it was also at bottom the cause of many of the mistakes and disappointments that followed in Reconstruction. It may be that emancipation could have come only through war, but it was also a very bad way for slaves to have their new birth of freedom. Military necessity during the fighting and the political ambition of the Republican party afterward were each in turn dominating elements in deciding what was best to be done for the freedmen. As a consequence blacks in the South became the target of all the embitterment and wounded pride of the defeated whites, who could say with some justice that blacks were being exploited against them and that the federal agencies were no more than fronts for northern vengeance and the Republican party. Ultimately the political corruption that obliterated the moral credit of the Republican state governments in the South was laid on the doorstep of the freedmen, who had little to do with it.

And so, when the excitement of the war and Reconstruction subsided, freedmen were left largely with what they had themselves made of their new freedom. For those with some advantages at the outset it certainly did mean an economic change of respectable dimension, landownership in the case of some; for blacks who had worked in hired-out positions even as slaves, it now meant that their paychecks were their own. One thinks of the ironworkers Charles Dew has studied in Virginia, who retained their former positions as free men instead of slaves.[21] One thinks of the meaning of freedom for a hired worker, who might have been "finding" his board and lodging with free blacks in some urban center and who now had the freedom he had only partially experienced in a practical sense before the war. For all of those "slaves without masters," the South's free blacks that Ira Berlin has written about, emancipation of slaves meant that the freedmen no longer had the burden of proving that they were free by carrying "free" papers.[22] For many field hands the "new birth in freedom" had been extremely painful after they had broken away from the plantation to join the throngs who followed the armies, facing the fatigue and hunger of forced marches and then the disease of contraband camps. For hundreds of these unfortunates, freedom meant death. A young agent of a freedmen's association vividly described the condition of a group of two hundred freedmen of both sexes and all ages who were sent back from North Carolina after having followed Sherman's army for several weeks. "Four men only were strong enough to carry up [the gangplank] those who could not lift a limb. Long, bony, and still, they lay along the decks, the flies swarming about them, as if they lit upon the dead. The silence of four was that of death; and before I had them all landed, the four were six. And yet their case has been that of thousands."[23] Smallpox and dysentery claimed many victims among these displaced persons. Most of the survivors probably in time found their way back to their home plantations to take their places with those who had never left or to take work on the farm of a man who had not been their owner. For these freedmen the revolution, and for us who would study it, was much harder to classify.

Yesterday's slave had accomplished two things whose importance it is easy to overlook. Two lordly opinions of racist whites were utterly confounded. Southern whites had often professed to believe that slaves were happier as slaves and that they had small wish for the responsibilities of freedom, and others, North and South, had freely predicted that blacks would never survive in a struggle with the powerful Anglo-Saxon majority. By deserting the plantation, by forming committees to voice their wish for the franchise or for participation in politics, they had shown that they preferred freedom and that they would survive.

One great result of emancipation was the loosening of old bonds of dependence. For the typical field hand freedom often meant that he had now to make decisions for himself within the circumscribed world of the plantation. He specifically resisted two things, living in the plantation quarters and working for wages at "gang" labor. He took up residence at some distance from the old "street" to work on a crop he could expect to divide with the owner, who would supply him with seed and equipment and land. For slaves of small farmers in the uplands, such a change was perhaps not very dramatic, but it must have seemed very great indeed to a man and his wife who had shared the communal life of the great plantations, rising at first light to the driver's horn, patterning a day in the field to the decisions of the owners, going and coming at the whim of the weather and the master, equally beyond challenge. For families who had been owned by several masters before 1863, it meant a mutual fireside for the first time.

The freedmen could now decide for themselves whether to work on the garden or the crop, which the weather and his own interests dictated as being best. A man often decided that his wife should no longer go to the field but should stay home and care for the children and tend the house and garden. If there were schools in the vicinity most freedmen wanted to take advantage of the opportunities afforded, but to do so meant losing the labor of older children, as it always has done for farmer folk. Which should come first, the present or the future? Under slavery there had never been anything but the present.

As Joel Williamson has pointed out, "freedom for the Negro in South Carolina was a growing thing, flowering in areas political historians have neglected." From his observations, this freedom came largely from its "operating within the organism itself. . . .

Thus, even in the early days of freedom former slaves with amazing unanimity revealed—by mass desertion, migration, idleness, by the breaching of the infinite minor regulations of slavery, by a new candor in relationships with whites, and by their ambition to acquire land—a determination to end their slavery."[24]

Bitter as the disappointments were that came with the reactions, painful as the readjustments were that had to be made outside the protection that the master's interests had provided in the old times, the record leaves small indication that many slaves yearned to have those old times back. The revolution, such as it was, was a revolution of hope and expectation. John Adams wrote of the American Revolution that it occurred in the minds and hearts of men before it was fought on the field, and there is a sense in which a thing cannot be fought for at the expense of life and limb until it has first been experienced. In that sense the Civil War and Reconstruction were only the beginning of a long revolution that blacks in time made for themselves, and it began with the necessity to think and act alone as individuals under the most adverse circumstances. It should be no surprise that it has required a very long time.

Blacks in that very long time built their own freedom, by drawing together as families and, yes, to a great extent by withdrawing, swiftly in some instances, slowly in others, from the institutions by which they had been integrated with the master's world. Why should the freedman stay in the white man's church when only whites could rise to leadership there? Through that black church the black leadership so sorely missed in Reconstruction slowly but surely developed. If most freedmen fell into the peonage of tenantry, some did not, and those who came to own their own land were examples to others less fortunate. We'd call them role figures today.

It strikes me as being less important what we call the emancipation—a revolution, an aborted revolution, or none at all—than how well we understand what really happened. All things are judged by comparison, after all. The historian's notion of slavery itself will have more than a little to do with the word he finally chooses for what happened between 1863 and 1876. The freedman certainly did not receive a whole loaf, not because he didn't want it, but because he was too weak at the time to establish a claim to it. But let us consider for a moment a thirsty citizen contemplating an eight-ounce glass with four ounces of water in it. One man might say the glass is half full, another that it is half empty. But, for the man who has been three days on a desert, four ounces are more than half as good as eight.

The first four ounces represent the possibility of there being a future. Although it would be foolish to claim too much for the Emancipation Proclamation, we should be humble enough to remember (those of us who have never known slavery) that the freedmen were overwhelmed with happiness in their "day of jubilee" and that they called freedom the jubilee because that celebration coming on the other side of Jordan was the only hope for future freedom they had had as slaves, the freedom beyond the grave. Which is just why they saw in the simple fact of freedom a veritable heaven on earth.

W. E. B. Du Bois as a Hegelian

JOEL WILLIAMSON

The experience of black people in America is personified in the experience of the mulatto. That experience is encapsulated in the lives of such people as W. E. B. Du Bois. He was neither black nor white; and yet he was both, floating between two worlds like a particle held in soft suspension, powerless either to find itself firmly settled upon the dark and solid bottom or to rise to a surface of light and air. Black America knows that experience.

It is almost as if the cultural experience of blacks in America has oscillated between a perfect separation from and a perfect integration with white culture, without ever achieving either. It is as if the closer black culture comes to either extreme the greater is the repelling force. It is much like a piston compressing air in a closed chamber or like the swinging of a pendulum —as the extreme is approached, an increasingly greater force is required to continue the approach. The result is that black culture seems to be suspended between the two poles, floating first one way and then the other. Yet "floating" does not capture the force of the dynamics that lie behind the movement. It is as if the suspension is caused by a near balance of powerful forces, always operating, some pushing black culture into what is commonly taken to be white, others pushing it toward an exclusive blackness.

In the American South, a cycle of integration began in 1619 when the first blacks entered Virginia, and it advanced rapidly in slavery. Transportation across the Atlantic itself deprived Afro-Americans of access to their ancestral culture. Afterwards, American slavery operated upon them like a forced-air furnace to burn out their natal culture and to melt them into the Western world. What began as a tearing away from place and people ended with a forced marriage to an aggressive and all-engrossing Western culture. If he survived in America, the black slave moved to integrate a new language, a new diet, a new religion, a new style of economics into his life. If he survived, he had moved significantly in the direction of whiteness. To some extent, the first integration was made easy in the South because the ratio of blacks to whites was quite small compared with what it would later become. For instance, as late as 1681 it was estimated that only some 4 percent of the population of Virginia was Negro. The first great influx of blackness appears to have come about 1730 and for two decades thereafter. Subsequently, race relations were almost a closed cultural terrarium; what grew came primarily from what was there, and very little of direct consequence came from the outside.

Between 1750 and 1831 black people, suspended between the black and white worlds, drifted slightly upward, becoming American more by their own impulses than by forced draft. Before this time, white America seems to have thought relatively little about slavery or blackness. It had made, as Winthrop Jordan phrased it, an "unthinking decision" to establish slavery. Now, the Revolutionary generation turned to face the twin issues of the disestablishment of slavery and the problem of blackness. It faced the issues only spottily, but with a focus and vigor not seen before. Possibly, this generation was the first to turn because it was the first to be born into an America that was rapidly becoming significantly black. In the South, some of the whites were born in seas of human darkness, but they all were faced with the necessity of calculating the far future of blackness in the new nation. What seems apparent in the mirror of history is that they barely managed to cope with slavery, to make the decision that tipped the balance of America ultimately in the direction of freedom. But they could not or would not decide about the meaning of blackness in human form. Whereas white America had begun in unthinking decision about slavery, it now passed to thinking indecision about blackness. In the white mind, there was an apparent ambivalence about black people, both in the broad world and in the bedrooms of the master class. The result was that the mixture of America tended to become lighter—both culturally and physically.

Frustrated, stymied, whites drifted until that heated August in 1831 when Nat Turner unilaterally denied them further indulgence. Slavery and blackness had to be dealt with because blacks, not whites, would have it so. Faced with the necessity of decision, the white world opted for slavery, probably a more stringent slavery than had existed before. The new slavery which existed in the South from the 1830s on might well be described as "hard-soft." It was hard in the sense that slave laws and black laws were made more strict, that the police forces to administer the laws were recast to execute a more perfect surveillance, and that the whole of the white community was enlisted in the effort of race control. It was soft in the sense that, in order to meet their fear of blackness, whites went among blacks in a new way, to tame them by making them white.

In the end, the whites were driving hard to create a whole and ordered society, an organic society, which had places and prescribed roles for white men, for white women, and for blacks. The organic society had not been fully achieved when the Civil War began. It was a shore dimly seen. But it was sighted by some, an important minority, who set the sails and held the rudder and captained the ship of southern culture. In the new order, blacks would be like white children who never grew old, and the whites would be perpetually patient paternalists. Blacks would be Sambos, childishly innocent, childishly thoughtless, playful, ingenious, lovable, even wise as youth is sometimes wise, but mostly physical, saved from their own extravagance by protecting fathers, prototypes of Robert E. Lee, who cared for his men so much, he said, "because they are under me." The ultimate result was that black culture rose to new heights of whiteness, to a new integration with the changing whole, which was itself becoming increasingly black. It is possible that the war accelerated the process of mixing black and white; certainly Reconstruction did so.

In Reconstruction, northern tutors took the places of southern ones in the education of black people. Where southerners had said to blacks, "So far and so high," northerners now seemed to say, "There is no limit to your whiteness; you too can be white as I am white." Black people were, it was often assumed, after all only white people with black skins. Blacks accepted the invitation eagerly, perhaps largely because they had already in slavery come so far along the road to whiteness. In freedom, they moved toward whiteness with certitude and an increasing rapidity. White America, an idealized white America, was what they sought, and they moved aggressively toward that goal.

Paradoxically and ironically, a perfectly black Reconstruction would have been very much white. If blacks had had all power in reconstructing the South, they would have created a world that was for the most part white, not black. What they sought was the realization of the ideals that they had been so diligently taught, in slavery and in freedom. The child was the father of the man. The child had become the adult, and he had learned—in a sense all too well—to obey the admonition: "Do as I say do, not as I do." Black ideals in Reconstruction were significantly white in economics, in politics, in education, and in matters of family and religion. They wanted farms and families, education in the classical style, and civil and religious equality. They sought to realize, in brief, the ideals that the dominant society projected. In seeking those goals, black legislators in the Reconstruction South easily outshone their white counterparts. And more, they tested all America upon its commitment to equality of citizenship. The South refused, essentially, to take the test. The North was not yet really prepared to take the test. When it did it faltered, it failed, and in 1877 it turned and walked away.

Painting the totality of black Reconstruction as very much white does not deny that, at the time of emancipation and continuously afterward, there was a rich culture distinctly black emerging from both the slave community and the free black worlds of North and South. There is now a rising tide of scholarship limning that separate black world, and it is producing a literature that is new and superbly valuable. That literature will ultimately, perhaps, wrench us usefully up and out of the well-worn grooves of the traditional conceptualization of slavery. Admittedly, much of what went on in black life in America began with the universals of human experience. For instance, there is a biology of family and kin that seems inevitable; there will be mothers and fathers and siblings and cousins in any society. But in the South, in these middle years of the nineteenth century, there were black variants of the universals. Indeed, a distinctively black culture can easily be seen in contemporary descriptions of dances, conjuring, folk songs and tales, music and musical instruments, religious practices and song, and the practice of medicine among black people. Moreover, the same accounts also quickly show that there were African survivals in these things as well as in language, burial rites, grave decorations, magic, and voodoo. Black people had even generated elements of a separate culture out of their very resistance to and sometimes rebelliousness against white culture. Ironically, sometimes the rebelliousness was against the denial to black people of equal access to white culture. Black culture was obviously not the same as white culture, and what was taken to be the dominant white culture was in reality significantly black; yet the ideal society that black people aspired to create during Reconstruction was fundamentally white. The fact that they did not then succeed indicates a lack of commitment to those ideals not by blacks, but by whites.

Scattered across the southern soil after Reconstruction, black people were aware of northern desertion and of their diminished ability to realize the white ideals. But they did not calculate the consequences of either. Increasingly apart from the white world physically, they persisted in the pursuit of whiteness. Inevitably, the vision blurred. Inevitably, what was sometimes thought to be white was really black. Furthermore, losing whiteness, like losing the sun-center of a solar system, produced a dispersal. Small black worlds spun out into space, where they became less and less relevant one to another. Black life fell precipitately away from whiteness, and as it fell it fragmented. Black life lost focus, it lost meaning, and it lost a measure of its capacity to give satisfaction to individual blacks.

White southerners saw the alienation, and many hastened to perfect it. These many moved away from an ideal of a place for black people in America toward one of no place for black people in America. Walled off from the white world, and, having no universe of its own, black life plunged toward what one black historian has called "the nadir of the Negro."

And then, over a space of decades, almost as if the physics of race relations in America had begun to work, the pendulum slowed, the piston stopped and began almost imperceptibly to reverse its motion. Booker T. Washington made the first stand. In Atlanta in 1895 he offered a compromise and made a bid for place. This far, this high on the white scale, he said, and we ask no more—a fingerhold on whiteness. In the twenty years of his life that followed, Washington organized black Americans vastly to achieve that end, to stand on the ragged edge of whiteness.

Some whites, remembering the "lost cause" and reviving the organic society, said in response, "Yes, of course, there is a place for the Negro." Other whites, looking to the future, said, "No, not even that. No place." Increasingly, as the years clicked over the turn of the century, more whites said no. The black belts said no. The five blackest states in the Deep South, then the heartland of race in America, where every other face was black with some to spare, said no emphatically and acted out their reply in lynchings, in riots, in legal segregation and disfranchisement, and in the whole broad circus of racial proscription. Never, never white was the message, overtly stated and everywhere made manifest.

If blacks could not be white, even a little bit white, what then would they be? Should they simply expire and dissolve themselves from the face of the American earth as white extremists might want? Should they settle for a little bit of whiteness as other whites and many blacks might want? Both were unhappy alternatives, one contrary to life itself, the other yielding a life perhaps not worth living.

Into the crisis, at the very hour of greatest need, there leapt a man with a solution. With astounding cogency, he stated the problem, the problem of not being able to achieve either whiteness or blackness in America. Then swiftly and deftly he raced around both horns of the dilemma to deliver a solution by posing, ironically, a parallel dilemma and its ideal solution. The man was not yet thirty when first he offered a way. He lived to be ninety-five, and he died just as his solution began to take palpable hold on the black mind in America and to take up a life of its own succeeding his life. The man was W. E. B. Du Bois. He was a mulatto, and he contained in his own slight body the central problem of black people in America. He, like they, was neither black nor white, yet he was both black and white. In posing the problem, Du Bois was stating his own problem, and in proposing the solution he was offering the solution he had constructed for himself. For Du Bois, the question of race was vastly personal. Because it was so personal, Du Bois's statement was so passionate; and because it was so passionate, it had strength and truth for black people in America.

After three years at Fisk University, four years at Harvard, and two at the University of Berlin, after teaching for a year at Wilberforce and researching and writing for a year at the University of Pennsylvania, Du Bois wrote in 1897 what is, perhaps, his most famous essay, eventually entitled "Of Our Spiritual Strivings."[1] I want to look at that essay again, to repeat the ideas it contains, and to speculate upon their sources and implications. In it Du Bois seems to do three things: he states the problem, he traces its origins, and he poses the solution.

Characteristically, Du Bois begins his essay with the statement of his own racial dilemma. With him, it began with his birth in Great Barrington, Massachusetts, in 1868. Of mulatto ancestry on both sides—and very light complexioned—he grew to consciousness in a community in western Massachusetts where blacks were few and far between. During his early life, he was hardly conscious of his darkness. Then, as he later recalled, the children of his crowd, all white and mostly well-to-do, decided to exchange visiting cards as did their elegant elders. It was a happy game and fun, for Will Du Bois as for the rest. But, of course, visiting cards were sometimes refused; and a "tall newcomer," a girl who perhaps did not understand the value of this slight, dark boy in the community, chose to play out that part of the role upon him. She refused his offered card, abruptly, "with a glance." With that refusal there dropped the "veil" between the superbly talented and highly sensitive young man and the great white world. Thereafter, for a time, he turned his energies into beating whites in every competition possible. But over the years his haughty contempt faded, and he found that all he wanted was white, all he wanted was theirs and not his. Attraction and repulsion left him floating between white and black. By 1897 when he published his article in *Century* magazine, he had found a solution for that problem for himself and for his people. In doing so he drew heavily upon the widely accepted concept that each people possessed a unique Volksgeist, a folk spirit, a germ implanted by God to be warmed to life in His own good time to play its part in the evolution of the history of the world. Du Bois had discovered the "souls of black folk."

"One ever feels his twoness,—an American, a Negro: two thoughts, two unreconciled strivings; two warring ideals in one dark body, whose dogged strength alone keeps it from being torn asunder," he wrote in that beautiful miniature of the black dilemma. He continued:

The history of the American Negro is the history of this strife, —this longing to attain self-conscious manhood, to merge his double self into a better and truer self. In this merging he wishes neither of the older selves to be lost. He would not Africanize America, for America has too much to teach the world and Africa. He would not bleach his Negro soul in a flood of white Americanism, for he knows that Negro blood has a message for the world. He simply wishes to make it possible for a man to be both a Negro and an American, without being cursed and spit upon by his fellows, without having the doors of opportunity closed roughly in his face.

This, then, is the end of his striving: to be a co-worker in the kingdom of culture, to escape both death and isolation, to husband and use his best powers and his latent genius.

Next Du Bois turned to explain how the problem had arisen. How had it happened that the black person in America had not been able to bring his potential genius to share in the development of culture? In Egypt, in Ethiopia, in the careers of certain black men, flashing briefly like falling stars, had appeared the shadow of a great past and of black genius. In America, in the relatively few days since emancipation, the black man's very power had been made to seem like weakness. "And yet it is not weakness," asserted Du Bois. It was, as he phrased it, "the contradiction of double aims." On the one side, black leaders had been led to drive their people to do white things, to hew wood and draw water. On the other side, black leadership had been able to see the dark genius only dimly. Black artists could not depict the beauty of black soul to whites because whites despised the black race. Black artists could not do white things because they were not white. This conflict of two souls had been devastating. On the one side, there was the soul of blackness, and, on the other, there was the genius of white America. "This waste of double aims," to quote Du Bois, "this seeking to satisfy two unreconciled ideals, has wrought sad havoc with the courage and faith and deeds of ten thousand people,—has sent them often wooing false gods and invoking false means of salvation, and at times has even seemed about to make them ashamed of themselves." As Du Bois saw the history, blacks in slavery had yearned after the ideal of freedom, in Reconstruction they had turned to pursue the new ideal of the ballot, and afterward they had turned still again to follow the idea of book learning. But it was white books and white learning that they sought—so long, so hard, and with so little profit.

And yet, even as they struggled after that last ideal, black people began to generate the solution to their dilemma: to discover the beauty of the souls of black folk as a thing in itself. The effort "changed the child of Emancipation," to use Du Bois's langauge again, "to the youth with dawning self-consciousness, self-realization, self-respect. . . . He began to have a dim feeling that, to attain his place in the world, he must be himself, and not another." As Du Bois saw it, out of evil came good; out of the very degradation of the Negro came the necessity of adjusting education more closely to real life, of focusing better his understanding of his social duties, and of realizing wherein lay real progress for himself. Thus dawned the age of, as Du Bois chose the phrase, "Sturm und Drang: storm and stress." Freedom, the ballot, book learning were not false ideals; they were simply incomplete, the "dreams of a credulous race childhood," or the aspirations of fond whites for blacks. Black folk needed all of these, argued Du Bois as he moved toward the heart of his solution,

not singly but together, not successively but together, each growing and aiding each, and all striving toward that vaster ideal that swims before the Negro people, the ideal of human brotherhood, gained through the unifying ideal of Race; the ideal of fostering and developing the traits and talents of the Negro, not in opposition to or contempt for the other races, but rather in large conformity to the great ideals of the American Republic, in order that some day on American soil two world-races may give each to each those characteristics both so sadly lack. We the darker ones come even now not altogether empty handed: there are to-day no truer exponents of the pure human spirit of the Declaration of Independence than the American Negroes, there is no true American music but the wild sweet melodies of the Negro slave; the American fairy tales and folk-lore are Indian and African; and, all in all, we black men seem the sole oasis of simple faith and reverence in a dusty desert of dollars and smartness.

Now allow me to attempt to translate Du Bois's presentation more explicitly. In the past experience of black people we have seen traces of black soul, but that genius, that spirit, is only now appearing on the stage of history. It is passing from childhood to young adulthood even now in 1897. In America, an oppressed black people has been constrained to pursue whiteness, ultimately a futile endeavor because black souls can never, of course, achieve whiteness. Yet out of the very struggle for and against whiteness, out of a rising absorption of whiteness, has come a rising consciousnes of blackness, and out of the negative of white rejection emerges the positive of black assertion. Thus blacks have found themselves truly different, and they have sensed that the difference is good. They are a child race, born of seed long latent and now in the proper moment of history warmed to life by a racial dialectic, black seed in a white pod, now bursting its shell and growing, nurturing itself on the substance of the very shell that had been both its shelter and its prison. The pursuit of blackness is the first and clear duty of black people, to search out and define their innate genius, the souls of black folk. By that, through that, they are moving toward the great ideal of human brotherhood. Ultimately blackness is not against whiteness, and ultimately two world races, black soul and white soul, will rise and join to realize the ideals of the American Republic. Thus it is that by getting out, by pursuing an exclusive blackness as they must, black people will get in. By looking inward, black people will move outward toward their ultimate destiny, and in that future all things—black and white—will be harmonious.

Du Bois's solution to the race problem in America was new, and it was revolutionary. Booker T. Washington could imagine no culture worth having that was not thoroughly laced with white ideals. Du Bois could boldly envision an evolution that began with a self-propelled withdrawal of black people from white culture and a plunge into pure blackness, yet still have faith that the two could harmoniously join farther down the stream of time. He did this, I suggest, by appropriating and adapting to the race problem in America late nineteenth-century idealism, especially Hegelianism and most especially Hegel's philosophy of history.

In what way was Du Bois's solution Hegelian? It was not, in fact, purely Hegelian. Significant portions of Hegel's thought were ignored, and had to be ignored. Hegel, who died in the 1830s, barely allowed subtropical Africans to walk onto his stage of history. Egypt was prominent but only as an extension of Persia, a connector between east and west.[2] Further, Hegel saw each people upon its own geography and its genius as springing from that geography. A poor climate and poor land would not produce a world historical people. One would not look to the polar areas or the tropics for greatness. "The true theatre of History is therefore the temperate zone," he declared, or rather its northern half, "because the earth there presents itself in a continental form, and has a broad breast, as the Greeks say."[3] Hegel did not envision a healthy mixing of races or world historical peoples. Indeed, each people had its innate genius, and a cultural mixing was essentially impossible. In the Hegelian universe, Du Bois himself was unreal; half-breeds had no place.

Du Bois was not purely Hegelian. In this as in other things, he was eclectic. Habitually, he surveyed the field of contemporary knowledge, and he used what he wanted, leaving strict logic to others. During this early stage of his professional life he seems to have had difficulty constructing tight and long-running rationales to undergird his writings. In 1890, his English instructor at Harvard caught his weakness in this respect precisely. "Unthinking seems to me the word for your style," he wrote. "With a good deal of emotional power, you blaze away pretty much anyhow. Occasionally, a sentence or a paragraph, and sometimes even a whole composition will be fine. Oftener there will be a nebulous, almost sulphorous [sic] indistinctness of outline. As for reserve of power, it is rarely to be found."[4] That was precisely the case with Du Bois's "Strivings" essay, with much of his writing, and with much of his life. Emotional power, not logic, was his strength.

It would be fruitless to search for a one-to-one appropriation of Hegelianism in Du Bois's essay; yet it is fundamentally Hegelian, and it is useful to consider it in that light. It is Hegelian in its language. The ten pages are heavily laden with favored Hegelian words such as *ideal, consciousness, strife,* and *self; spirit, soul,* and *genius; conflict* and *contradiction; freedom* (three times with a capital *F*), and *folk.* Most interesting and relevant is his appropriation of the Hegelian view of history. Du Bois, like Hegel, sees the history of the world as the spirit of freedom rising to realize itself through specific world historical peoples. Consciousness is not achieved individually and one by one, but rather through whole peoples, each people rising to a consciousness of itself, pursuing its Volksgeist, its spirit, its soul, its genius. God implanted in each people a distinct seed, and that essence, that spirit, struggles for life with its opposite, matter. As it struggles, as it exercises its will, it rises and matures, unfolding the full promise that was always there, pre-formed, latent in the seed. On earth, life is filled with confusion and conflict and contradiction. But they are all working toward a rising communion of man with the Godhead. All soul, all spirit, all truth and reality ultimately are emanations of God's mind. In His mind all is harmonious, all is one, all things are unified, and there are no contradictions. As each people rises to know its true self, it rises closer to God—to true freedom and to each other. If we seem so separated on earth, it is because we do not yet fully know ourselves and, hence, God. Inevitably we shall do so. "The History of the World is none other than the progress of the consciousness of Freedom," Hegel declared.[5]

In beginning courses in philosophy, the Hegelian idea of progress is often described as moving by the thesis-antithesis-synthesis-thesis model. At a given time a given society is complete within itself and relatively static. Then, as that society slowly matures, it breeds out of its own self a contradiction, an opposite, an antithesis. The antithesis grows and overwhelms the thesis but does not totally erase it. Rather it takes the essence of the thesis, the best of the old, and marries it to the new in a synthesis. In still more time, vestigal contradictions between the two systems peel away, and a new thesis is formed. Shortly, Karl Marx revised Hegel by arguing that material changes create the antithesis, but Hegel preached that the prime mover comprised ideas, ideas contrary to the old order first grasped from that very order by "world historical men." New ideas are the engines that move men forward through history toward God. Thus Christ came with a new idea, which grew out of an old order, Christianity overthrew the old order, and yet it saved the essence of the old and married it to itself. Christianity moved man up a notch closer to God. More recently, the German nations had moved through Christianity to know the truth that man is innately free and to point the way toward ultimate salvation.[6]

Du Bois neatly pressed the Negro American into the Hegelian model. Hegel traced the world spirit as having moved forward toward a realization of itself through the successive histories of six world historical peoples: Chinese, Indians, Persians (culminating in the Egyptians), Greeks, Romans, and Germans.[7] Du Bois brought on the Negro as "a sort of seventh son, born with a veil, and gifted with second-sight in this American world."[8] Hegel had not treated the temperate zone of North America with depth because, he said, that was the future and he was concerned with history.[9] Du Bois stood ready to fill out the story quickly, inserting black folk into North America and drawing out the Hegelian dialectic with a heavy hand. Out of American Negro slavery itself had come freedom, he declared. The freedom that black folk in America came to know was newer and richer than any known before, because "few men ever worshiped Freedom with half such unquestioning faith as did the American Negro for two centuries." Out of slavery and out of the later striving of black folk for whiteness in an oppressive white world came a rising sense of black soul. "The child of Emancipation" became the "youth with dawning self-consciousness, self-realization, self-respect. In those sombre forests, of his striving his own soul rose before him, and he saw himself,—darkly as through a veil. . . . He began to have a dim feeling that, to attain his place in the world, he must be himself, and not another."[10] Thus it was that white thesis bred black antithesis, which took the best of the white and moved it upward toward a new synthesis. The whiteness that was in black Americans—the realization of the ideal of freedom, of civil rights, of white book learning—was a good thing. It had brought blackness to life and had nurtured it. Du Bois would not erase white learning from black minds. Rather would he nurture the newfound blackness both with and against whiteness. Out of the racial dialectic would come an eventual harmony. Thus, what appears to us on earth as conflict and strife—"two souls . . . two . . . strivings; two warring ideals"—are but the working out of the Hegelian program. What seems an insoluble problem is, in Hegelian dialectics, a solution in progress. One only adds faith and will. The move toward self-conscious blackness had begun, and it would run its inevitable course. When black people know their souls, they will know truth, beauty, and the ultimate reality, God. When they know themselves, they too will know whiteness, and they will be at peace with the whiteness that is within them. In America, black and white will finally join together in rising harmony and unity to make a better nation, to form a new thesis in which human brotherhood and human freedom will more perfectly reign.

Begging the question for the moment and assuming that beneath the sulfurously smoking words Du Bois was offering a basically Hegelian solution to the race problem in America, let me now speculate on how Du Bois became a Hegelian.

When Du Bois went to Fisk in the fall of 1885, he was already committed to accepting black folk as his own in spite of his northernness and his own light skin. From the time that the "tall newcomer" had snubbed him and the veil had dropped,

Du Bois cultivated his alienation as an asset. "I had thereafter no desire to tear down that veil, to creep through; I held all beyond it in common contempt, and lived above it in a region of blue sky and great wandering shadows," he recalled. "The sky was bluest when I could beat my mates at examination-time, or beat them in a foot-race, or even beat their stringy heads."[11] His family and white friends resented the fact that the local whites who sponsored his education were sending him south. But Will welcomed the opportunity. He realized that at home he was falling into a "spiritual isolation," and he saw in the South a chance to join his own. At dinner on the night of his arrival at Fisk he was "deliriously happy" to sit across the table from "two of the most beautiful beings God ever revealed to the eyes of 17." One of these was Lena Calhoun, the great-aunt of the actress Lena Horne and, according to Du Bois, "far more beautiful." He gloried in the beauty and strength of his schoolmates, and for two summers he went out to teach black children in rural Tennessee. At Harvard he continued to accept himself "as a member of a segregated caste."[12]

There are signs that at Fisk Du Bois had already begun to think in Hegelian terms. Philosophy under President Ernest Cravath had been his favored subject. At Harvard, he recalled, "above all I wanted to study philosophy!" He chose to take a course in ethics with George Herbert Palmer.[13] Palmer was the chairman of the department and a popular lecturer; but most of all he was a profound and devoted Hegelian, one of those scholars who promoted a revival of Hegelianism in the United States in the 1880s.[14] Du Bois could hardly avoid the Hegelian in academic America, and it was a philosophy that was congenial to his nature and his needs. He always combined, like America at large in his lifetime, a paradoxical teaming of the ideal and the real, the romantic and the pragmatic. At Harvard he further refined and combined each of the two.

It happened that Palmer went on sabbatical, and Du Bois took his first philosophy course under William James.[15] James was in the process of developing his "pragmatic philosophy." As yet, he had not so much developed a philosophy as he had an opposition, including a loyal and loving opposition to such idealism represented by Palmer's Hegelianism.[16] As his young colleague George Santayana noted, James had a "love of lame ducks and neglected possibilities."[17] That certainly gave Du Bois two votes from James. James invited Du Bois several times to his home and became, as Du Bois remembered, "my friend and guide to clear thinking."[18] During his first year at Harvard, Du Bois also counted among his favorite professors Nathaniel Southgate Shaler, a protégé of Louis Agassiz. Shaler was a natural scientist whose class in basic geology attracted hundreds of students.[19] A central theme of his teaching was the great age of the earth and the presence of man on earth. He taught that each people had distinctive traits that were deeply grooved in time and were set almost before history began. Later he published a book about black people, alleging that they were born with certain traits. Among these he stressed their spiritual and musical natures.[20] Shaler, a Kentuckian and son of a slaveholder, was also very sympathetic to Du Bois. He expelled a student from his class who objected to sitting next to Du Bois. The professor explained that the expelled scholar "wasn't doing very well, anyway."[21]

In his second year, Du Bois studied French and German philosophy with Santayana, then an instructor fresh from studies at the University of Berlin. In the same year, he earned an A+ in history from Albert Bushnell Hart. Hart had himself appropriated from the Germans the seminar method of graduate instruction along with a faith that the scientific study of the institutions of a people would reveal the nature of their fundamental genius. Hart was fascinated by the race problem in America, and he took a special interest in young Du Bois.[22] At the end of his senior year, in his commencement oration,

Du Bois combined philosophy and history. In a tight, neat dialectic, he pitted the arrogant, aristocratic Jefferson Davis as the logical product of the institutions of antebellum southern culture against an opposite pole of "the patient, trustful, submissive African as a type of citizen the world would some day honor."[23]

A graduate student in his third year, Du Bois adopted an activist method he would long pursue, that of the social science researcher. He would study the Negro scientifically, he resolved, and find the truth beneath the black experience. Even as he continued to refine the idealistic side of his philosophy, Du Bois evolved a realistic side. One might spend his life in that "lovely but sterile land of philosophic speculation." He had wanted to do just that before he met James and Hart. But James convinced him that philosophy paid but poorly, and Hart not only opened the way for him to a profession, but he also trained him in the social science method, which would give substance to his philosophy. "After my work with Hart in United States history," he recalled in his autobiography, "I conceived the idea of applying philosophy to an historical interpretation of race relations."[24] At Hart's suggestion, he began that work with his doctoral dissertation on the suppression of the African slave trade to America.[25]

In the fall of 1892, Du Bois went abroad to study. In Europe he met racial prejudice, but there were significant times when he seemed able to let his blackness go and to appreciate the fact that "white folk were human."[26] Perhaps by freeing himself of the white devil, he was enabled to see more clearly a black folk independent of whiteness. Europe also seemed to give Du Bois an appreciation of the contemporary world. Nationalistic, capitalistic, and industrializing, white Europe was rapidly devouring the colored world, from South Africa to Samoa, from Singapore to Siberia. That great fact did not escape the young scholar.

In Germany, Du Bois chose to study in the University of Berlin. Perhaps it is not significant that Berlin was the university where Hegel himself had brought his great career to a close three generations before. It is significant, however, that when Du Bois arrived Berlin was in the midst of a Hegelian revival. Among those under whom he studied in his first semester was Heinrich von Treitschke, perhaps the most famous of the neo-Hegelians. Du Bois was deeply impressed by the great Teuton. "To me by far the most interesting of the professors is the well-known von Treitschke," he wrote in his diary.[27]

On the eve of his twenty-fifth birthday, February 23, 1893, Du Bois performed a solitary and singular ceremony, which suggests that he had absorbed a large and rather pure dose of Hegelianism. Alone in his room he made, as he said in his diary, a "sacrifice to the Zeitgeist." He conjured with candles, wine, oil, song, and prayer and dedicated his library to his long-dead mother. Finally, he turned to his diary. "I am glad I am living," he wrote. "I rejoice as a strong man to run a race, and I am strong—is it egotism, is it assurance—or is it the silent call of the world spirit that makes me feel that I am royal and that beneath my sceptre a world of kings shall bow." He resolved to live his life to the fullest, declaring, "Its end is its greatest and fullest self—this end is the Good. The Beautiful its attribute— its soul and Truth is its being." Perhaps the candle was still flickering against the cold winter night as he resolved to live for the good of his black brothers and sisters, and for the world's good. The latter he could not define. "I therefore," he vowed, "take the work that the Unknown lays in my hands & work for the rise of the Negro people, taking for granted that their best development means the best development of the world." Du Bois paused, then he concluded. "These are my plans: to make a name in science, to make a name in literature and thus to raise my race. Or, perhaps to raise a visible empire in Africa thro' England, France, or Germany."[28]

It is possible, then, that by 1893 Du Bois saw himself potentially as one of Hegel's world historical men, a dark messiah to lead his people toward salvation. In June of 1888 his commencement oration at Fiske had been upon Otto von Bismarck, a man who by his own will and strength "had made a nation out of a mass of bickering peoples."[29] More recently, he had felt the thundering Pan-Germanism of Treitschke. Du Bois as black Bismarck was conceivable in Hegelian terms, for salvation existed in a new idea, realized by a very special man. As Hegel explained, there are ideas whose times have come. A "*creating* Idea," a truth striving toward consciousness of itself, will come to light in the personal ambition of a world historical person. Hegel offered the example of Caesar, whose great ambition served his people even as it served Caesar. "Such are all great historical men," asserted Hegel, "whose own particular aims involve those large issues which are the will of the World Spirit." Historical men move from an "inner Spirit which, impinging on the outer world as on a shell, burst it to pieces, because it is another kernel than that which belonged to the shell in question." These people are heroes; their visions, their deeds, their words signify the essence of their times; and their fellows listen because they hear and they know in their hearts that the hero speaks the truth for that epoch. No happy hearts are heroes. Their lot is a life of strife, of struggle, of essential and profound unhappiness, and then, as Hegel said, "they die early, like Alexander; they are murdered, like Caesar; transported to St. Helena, like Napoleon."[30] It was not the fate of Du Bois to suffer the great end, though he courted both suffering and the great end. He did not die early but late, he was not murdered perhaps because we had not yet learned in America routinely to kill our heroes, and we would not even force him into exile. But he could take himself off to Africa at last, as he did, and he could have an essentially unhappy and tragic life, as he also did.

Thus Hegel gave Du Bois a philosophy and a purpose in life—both of which he very much and complexly needed. Hegel also gave him a formula for working his way out of a difficult situation for himself and for black people. In the real world whites were not accepting blacks as whites, and the prospects were that they never would. If black life was to have meaning, to have value, it would have to be a separated life and value. If black people were to find values for themselves, those values would have to be black and tied to a separate black culture. Du Bois used Hegelianism to rationalize a way around the white wall, to legitimate its existence and its exclusiveness, without devaluing himself or his people. In its meanest possibility, Du Bois's system was an evasion of reality; it was a way of coping with the outrageous oppression of blacks in American life. Like an earlier evasion of magnificent proportions, it asserted that the city of God was in heaven rather than in Rome. It was more a formula for survival than for prosperity. It was a philosophical system constructed to obviate an outrageous reality and a way of dealing mentally with impossible and omnipresent oppression.

Still asuming that this analysis is basically true, what are its uses? What does it add to what we already know? First, it adds something to the picture of Du Bois as a black leader. It seems that in 1893 Du Bois saw himself as destined for great things as a leader of his race, perhaps even as the world historical man who would lead his people onto the stage to play their destined role in the progress of mankind. This sense of mission shaped his attitude toward other black leaders. In 1891 he alluded to the venerable Frederick Douglass as a "time server."[31] In 1903, at the age of thirty-five and as a professor at Atlanta University, he challenged Booker Washington and the Tuskegee machine. Washington had other opponents; it was Du Bois, however, who took the lead in the opposition, not with a machine, not with an organization, but with an idea—the souls of black folk. Du Bois's strength in the combat lay in the breadth of his intellect. He was tremendously sophisticated. He was as complex as the world civilization from which he sprang, and thus he was superbly well armed to deal with that world. In philosophy, his idealism encompassed his realism, and it also encompassed Washington and the Tuskegee idea. Du Bois could go as far as Washington, and he could also go farther. When his program began to fail, Washington had no great alternative. As a realist, he could only deal with what was. As an idealist, Du Bois could deal not only with what was but also with what ought to be. Du Bois could absorb reality, and he could transcend it. It was not inevitable that the two men should have differed. Indeed, for several years they did not. It is conceivable that, if the Tuskegee idea had worked well enough, Du Bois would never have raised the idealistic alternative. But increasingly after 1900, as lynchings and riots continued, as legal disfranchisement and segregation proceeded, it became clear that southern Negroes under Washington's leadership were rapidly losing ground, especially in the Deep South. For Du Bois the switch to the idealistic alternative was almost automatic.

Philosophically, Booker T. Washington was essentially a realist. He looked to the visible, palpable world of truth. He concluded that black culture was separate from white only in that it was denied access to whiteness. There was no separate and beautiful integrity in blackness itself. Du Bois, on the other hand, began as an idealist. For him ultimate truth and ultimate reality existed in the realm of ideas. Once he assumed that color was culture, he permanently separated black from white, in America and elsewhere. Washington never made that assumption. On the contrary, he seemed to assume that blacks could be and ought to strive to be totally white culturally. But Du Bois's idealism, like that of many of his contemporaries, was complemented by a host of practical programs. Thus he could wholeheartedly endorse industrial education for the mass of black youths and sometimes seem very like Washington in that stance.

Further, if one remarks Du Bois's messiah complex, one understands his loneliness, even among the most sympathetic of black and white American liberals, his aloofness, and his final alienation. The role prescribed such isolation, and Du Bois seemed determined, often perversely, to achieve it. The role also prescribed suffering, and he sought that too. In a smooth mixture of Christian and Hegelian metaphors, he painted himself in *Dusk of Dawn* as being "crucified on the vast wheel of time" while "he flew round and round with the zeitgeist."[32]

Also, Hegelianism was easily turned into Marxian socialism. As Marx declared, he found Hegel standing on his head, and he set him aright. Setting him aright consisted of substituting material or economic engines for ideational ones. Du Bois's pursuit of the scientific method in studying the Negro problem inevitably brought him into contact with the pervasive power of economic motivation. He was early attracted to socialism, but he was also soon repelled by the racism of socialists. Ultimately, he was probably always more Hegelian than Marxist, more black than socialist. If Hegel was upside-down, then Du Bois seemed comfortable standing on his head.

When seen in the frame of Hegelianism, Du Bois's turn in the 1930s to the "self-segregation" of blacks was not, as critics charged, a giving up of the struggle for equal rights in America or a reversal of previous directions. It was rather a reasonable reaction to black folk losing their souls to whiteness in the despair of the Depression. It is more of Du Bois's steady idea that only by realizing their own genius can black people share fully in America. Only by getting out can they get in.

Black soul led inevitably to black Africa. Blacks all over the world were bound together by blackness, and mother Africa was home. If, as Hegel said, the history of the world is the struggle of the world spirit through world historical peoples to realize the principle that every one is free; if, as he suggested, each great people has its special geography; and if, as Du Bois declared, the black race is the seventh and next world historical people, then Africa is the place where freedom will reach its next and highest level. "Africa," he wrote in 1924, "is the Spiritual Frontier of human kind."[33] Thus, the preservation and the promotion by all blacks of mother Africa, of Pan-Africanism, became highly important. In the end he would go there and make his home where blackness began.

Finally, and by far most important, is that Du Bois's Hegelianism led him into generating what appears to be one of the lasting polar positions through which black people interpret themselves in America. Du Bois was the first of the soul brothers, and he was more than that—he was the Christ of the soul movement, the man with the saving idea. Very much as if he were acting out that messianic complex evinced on his twenty-fifth birthday, he came forth with the idea that was to save his people. He was the first to provide a large and satisfying philosophy, which declared that not only is black present and innate and that black blood means black culture (which is not and never can be white culture), but also that black is God-given and beautiful. Far from erasing black culture and merging black folk into white culture, he would cultivate and preserve its uniqueness.

This brings us back to where we began. Like black people in America, Du Bois was both black and white, culturally as well as physically. He was at war with himself, in himself, as were black people. To be black and to be American seemed a contradiction because America seemed white. With the concept of black soul he was able to transcend the apparent contradiction. He was black and he was American and each of these was valuable. True blackness, when realized, would incorporate the best of the white American experience and rise to new heights of beauty in the very process of overcoming whiteness.

The soul movement had its strong beginnings with Du Bois. The early movement had its pharisees and its Herod. It had its heresies and its apostates and, later, its Renaissance and its Reformation. Even recently, white America seems to be in the process of granting the soul movement an edict of toleration. It seems highly probable that the Church Black, like the Church White, is here to stay. If we would better understand the Church Black, the cult of soul, we might lay the template of Hegelianism upon it. One can understand the special passion of the soul movement in the late 1960s to include all of the brothers and sisters, if he knows that in the Hegelian system souls are not purely single, that they suffer the flesh, that they are liable to be overwhelmed by the world of matter unless they realize their true lives in a spiritual communion with other like souls, in this case with the souls of black folk. Black people who do not join the communion are beyond the pale, cut off from the warming light of being, doomed to wander the earth like zombies, as flesh without soul, to suffer not simply isolation and death, but unreality and nonbeing. Salvation lies only and ultimately in the Church Black, and all without are doomed.

Du Bois died in 1963. If he had lived another decade, he would probably have viewed the progress of events in America with great satisfaction. He would have seen black consciousness move up yet another round on the Hegelian spiral. The civil rights movement struggled against white oppression. It made its mark upon the white world, but it made a greater mark on the black world. Out of the very denial of whiteness, out of the denial of Americanness, out of the continuing oppression of neo-slavery, came black self-assertion. In the stress, in the struggle, in the storm to get into whiteness, black people rediscovered blackness. To merge oneself into whiteness, to be a perfectly white American, would have been death and denial. In the storm and stress of trying to get in, black people learned that they had to get out, that their first duty was to know themselves.

"We shall overcome" became "black is beautiful." Black people struggled, and they rose to a newer and higher awareness of self—an awareness that now could never be denied, never reversed, that would always be a part of what is to come. Du Bois, more than any other person, gave black people in America the concept of soul as a way of organizing their lives. In doing so he gave them a vital and enduring idea that not only gave them a present but also a past and a promising future.

Du Bois left a great legacy to black people, but he also left something of value to white Americans. If one is white and American, appreciating the idea of black soul is a way of understanding one's white self better. Lamentably, white people had no Du Bois to call forth their better selves in ethnic terms; their whiteness had focus, but it was horribly and tragically directed against other races. Yet, around the turn of the century, a few thoughtful whites borrowed from Hegelianism and Western idealism for their own purposes just as had Du Bois. The structures that they built, especially in the black South, were not unlike those of Du Bois. There was an evolution of white soul and the Church White that paralleled black soul and the Church Black. Popular education, popular religion, popular politics, a warming interest in Appalachian and swampland folklore as deep-freeze depositories of Anglo-Saxon genius, and a number of other phenomena were all, in part, conscious attempts to realize the genius that was white. What might well be called Volksgeistian conservatism was abroad in the land, and it left deep and indelible marks upon both black and white culture in the twentieth century.

It was no mere coincidence that those who led in the Church White were those who cared most for the souls of black folk. Often enough, those who cared launched efforts to help the Negro. When those efforts failed, they turned their attention to the elevation of their white brothers and sisters. Edgar

Gardner Murphy, for example, was a pioneer opponent of lynching in the 1890s, organized the Montgomery Race Conference in 1900, and concerted the only full-scale attempt by southern conservatives to deal with the race problem during these turn of the century years. When that failed, he turned his energies to ending the cultural crippling of white children by pressing them into the factories for most of their waking lives. From that, he passed on to crusade for the universal, free, and compulsory education of the children of the South. He would bring into the culture those who were heretofore, as he worded it, "non-participants." As Murphy and the Volksgeistians saw it, segregation was necessary to salvation for both blacks and whites. Whites could not save blacks, and they might confuse them. The souls of black folk could only be saved by black folk. The duty of white leadership lay primarily in the cultivation of a communion among white saints.

On the white side of the race line, the spiritual heirs of the Volksgeistian conservatives are the thoughtful activists in the civil rights movement of recent years. Like their cultural progenitors, they began by struggling for blackness, and they ended by finding, in some degree, a higher and better whiteness. It was in the civil rights movement that many whites unwittingly found their souls, in striving with blacks against the white wall, in conflict with the soulless flesh of affluence, and ultimately in rejection at the hands of their erstwhile black colleagues. In the mid-1960s, whites who would marry blackness in the movement were denied blackness by blacks. Of necessity, like the Volksgeistians more than a half-century before, they were forced to turn back upon themselves and to turn inward. And yet the rejection has not been easily absorbed. Whites who somehow still feel the tug of blackness, whites who care about black people because they are we, as we are they, feel the twoness, the two as yet unreconciled strivings, the two warring ideals in our own light bodies, and we too have faith that we have the strength that will keep us from being torn asunder.

The tension that self-conscious white souls feel today is unthinkingly shared by all white America. White is indeed married to black by national geography and by centuries of time. More important, they are married because each has given to each so much, and taken so much. Black America is so much white; and white America, in its stubborn and residual egotism, is only slowly realizing how very black it is, and has been. The strife against that awareness, the rage against realization, is our struggle. How does it feel to be a problem—a white problem? It is agony, it is storm and stress, it is to clatter about on the edge of perdition, the earth falling away even as we raise each foot for the next step. But it is also to strive, to struggle, and to have faith that from our spiritual strivings will emerge a sense of self that will be truer, that will be stronger, that will give us meaning and a measure of peace, that will indeed give us the "souls of white folk."

Sharecropping: Market Response or Mechanism of Race Control?

RICHARD SUTCH & ROGER RANSOM

Economists have for some time been interested—*fascinated* might be a more apt word—in the structure and performance of the economy of the American South during the early nineteenth century. The initial effort in 1958 by Alfred Conrad and John Meyer to measure the "profitability" of antebellum slavery produced a vigorous debate.[1] Originally, the economists who turned their attention to this issue felt they were settling a long-standing debate among historians by bringing more sophisticated economic analysis to bear on the problem. But it soon became apparent that the historical issues were more subtle and complex than first formulated. The debate expanded into a general discussion of the viability of the slave economy and the nature of southern economic development. The publication in 1971 of a collection of essays, written by both historians and economists, on the question "Did slavery pay?" served to demonstrate that the investigation into the full range of historical issues had only begun.[2] Indeed, several economists had by that time launched full-scale investigations into the slave economy. Robert Gallman, William Parker, and their students concentrated on the structure of the antebellum southern economy, production relationships, interregional trade flows, distribution of wealth, and related topics.[3] Recently Robert Fogel and Stanley Engerman have offered a highly controversial economic analysis of the welfare of enslaved Negroes based on their seven-year study of American slavery.[4] A vigorous response by their critics has already produced yet another round of investigations.[5]

This intense interest in the economic analysis of slavery has recently spawned a parallel interest in emancipation and its economic consequences. The American experience with emancipation has attracted particular attention not only because it was the most direct and far-reaching action ever undertaken to end slavery, but also because the economic aspects of this history raise some crucial questions.[6] One of them concerns the origins and functions of sharecropping.

There is no question that the freeing of four million slaves initiated an economic transformation of enormous proportions. Abolition of chattel labor destroyed the economic basis of the old plantation society. As a result, the entire structure of the southern economy had to be reshaped. Before the Civil War, most staple production was carried out by slave work gangs on large plantations. Supervised in every detail by drivers, slaves on these plantations served as a highly organized and disciplined labor force that operated what one scholar describes as "factories in the field."[7] The large plantations, although generally self-sufficient in their food needs, maintained elaborate financial and marketing arrangements with urban banks, cotton factors, and commission merchants, who looked after the financing and annual provisioning of the agricultural operation and the marketing of the resulting output.

Within a few years following the war, all this had changed. In place of the large plantations were tens of thousands of small-scale tenant farms. Each of these small farms, which rarely comprised more than forty acres of cultivated land, was invariably operated by a single family. Frequently their tenancy was a form known as sharecropping. The farm family did not, for the most part, produce its own food; southern tenants concentrated on growing cotton and purchased corn and pork from local retail merchants. The large financial intermediaries disappeared, and the underwriting and marketing of the cotton crop were taken over after the war by the rural merchants. There were literally thousands of these country stores, each serving a limited clientele in its own neighborhood.

The disappearance of the plantation system and the reallocation of land to black tenant farmers were perhaps the most visible of these dramatic changes. Indeed, it is hardly an exaggeration to say that the rise of sharecropping is symbolic of the economic revolution that swept the South after 1865. With sharecropping, the output of the farm was equally divided between labor and the landlord. This might at first seem to be a straightforward economic transaction, but, as the title of our essay suggests, sharecropping has come to be viewed as an exploitative economic relationship and a mechanism of social control. If so, it immediately becomes a puzzle to explain how such an institution could have arisen in response to the shock of emancipation. Was sharecropping forcibly imposed on blacks as a substitute for slavery? Or was the interaction between economic and social forces more complex? In this essay we seek answers to such questions as: Why did this form of tenure, which was virtually unknown before the Civil War in the South, become so common among blacks after the war? What did sharecropping mean to the men and women who chose it (or were forced to choose it)? What contribution did sharecropping make to the economic progress of the South and, in particular, to the economic welfare of the black population of the South? Finally, was sharecropping merely a market institution, or was it a mechanism of race control?

Before we turn to these questions, however, several general points need to be clarified. First, it is important to emphasize that sharecropping was not the universal (or even the most prevalent) method of managing farms in the American South

TABLE 1   Tenure and Race of Farm Operators in the Cotton South, 1880

Tenure	Percentage Distribution of Farms			Percentage of Total Acreage in Crops in Each Class		
	White	Black	All	White	Black	All
Owned	41.3	7.3	48.6	51.0	9.8	60.8
Rented	4.8	9.6	14.4	6.7	6.9	13.6
Share-cropped	16.6	20.3	37.0	11.8	13.8	25.6
All Farms	62.7	37.3	100.0	69.5	30.5	100.0

SOURCE: Roger Ransom and Richard Sutch, *One Kind of Freedom: The Economic Consequences of Emancipation* (New York: Cambridge University Press, 1977), Tables 4.3 and 5.1, pp. 69 and 84.

NOTE: The precise definition of the cotton South and procedures used to select farms from the census records of this region are detailed in Appendix G of the source. Briefly, it can be noted that the sample comprises farms from the cotton-growing regions of North Carolina, South Carolina, Georgia, Florida, Alabama, Mississippi, Louisiana, and Texas.

following the Civil War. Table 1 presents data on tenure and the race of farm operators in the cotton South in 1880. It reveals that only 37 percent of southern farms, accounting for about 25 percent of all acreage reported in crops, was sharecropped; whereas about half of all farms, with 60 percent of the acreage in crops, were owner-operated enterprises. Nonetheless, sharecropping was more significant in determining the economic future of the former slaves than these aggregate figures might suggest. Most of the owner-operated farms described in the table were small enterprises that had been operated at that scale by their white owners before the war. Over one-half (54 percent) of all black farmers were sharecroppers. Put another way, three-quarters (73 percent) of the farms that were *not* sharecropped were managed or owned by whites.

Sharecropping was, moreover, the form of agricultural organization that replaced the antebellum plantation. Such plantations had completely disappeared by 1880. We did not find a single plantation-sized farm in that year among the five thousand individual southern farms for which we examined the census records.[8] In fact, over 99 percent of all farms we examined reported less than two hundred acres in crops. Contemporaries frequently observed that land that before the war had been organized into plantations was being extensively sharecropped after the war. A survey of planters taken in 1868–1869 showed that 80 percent of their land was sharecropped.[9] Robert Somers observed in 1871 that sharecropping prevailed "so generally that any other form of contract is but the exception."[10]

A second fact, which is sometimes overlooked, is that sharecropping did not immediately emerge as a substitute for the plantation. As we shall argue shortly, this new form of tenure appeared only after several years of experimentation with a variety of alternative arrangements and after determined efforts by planters to reimpose the familiar gang-labor system had failed. In 1865 and 1866, sharecropping contracts were so rare that, when one was encountered, contemporaries referred to it as an "experiment" or as an "undeveloped idea."[11] To be sure, the idea developed quickly. As we have noted, by the end of the 1860s observers were commenting on the prevalence of sharecropping.

Our third clarification is the need to distinguish what is commonly called sharecropping from the share-wage system. Immediately after the war, planters generally attempted to cultivate their plantations with gang labor, which was to be paid monthly wages. In many areas, a shortage of working capital and credit prevented planters from paying wages in cash. One way of overcoming this problem was to give the labor either a fixed amount of the crop or a share of the output once the harvest was completed. Obviously, the system of paying wage laborers with a share of the crop is not a form of tenancy. In any case, the practice became less common as credit conditions improved and U.S. currency began to circulate. Sharecropping, remunerating tenants with a fixed share of the harvest, on the other hand, is a form of tenancy. The landlord agreed to provide the land, housing, fuel, workstock, feed for stock, farming implements, and seed. The cropper and his family agreed to work the land and to feed and clothe themselves. Whenever these terms were agreed to, the common-law stipulation that output be divided equally applied. There were other tenancy contracts that involved sharing of output, but none were very common. The fifty-fifty split was the nearly universal form of working upon shares.

What explains the widespread adoption of sharecropping?
The most obvious effect of abolishing slavery was that landowners lost their physical control over labor. The basis of the work-gang system had been compulsion. Slave drivers set a steady and demanding pace throughout the day. Thoroughness was expected of each gang member and, if necessary, was enforced by the lash. Without the complete control over labor inherent in the slave-master relationship, the high productivity of the antebellum work gang could not have been maintained.[12] Of course, removal of coercion need not have led planters to discard the work gang. One can imagine this system (which was the only one familiar to planters in 1865) continuing in the postwar period even though output per man would have been reduced. Imaginative planters might even have contrived financial incentives to replace the lash and thus restore at least some of the efficiency lost through the absence of control.

In fact, this is precisely what planters invariably tried. They employed hired workers organized in gangs similar to the old system. But those attempts failed. This was largely because of another reaction to emancipation: the sharp contraction in the supply of labor offered by blacks. Slavery was a system of extreme exploitation—indeed, in the American case, nearly total exploitation—of labor. Black slaves received only enough food, clothing, and shelter to keep them healthy and hardworking. Theirs was truly a "subsistence" wage. This, after all, is why slaves were worth so much to planters; between 54 and 60 percent of their labor product was expropriated by the master.[13] This degree of exploitation implies that, once they became free, former slaves could have more than doubled their material income. But freedom also allowed blacks to determine how they wished to spend their time. Not surprisingly, once free they elected to work less than they had as slaves, when men, women, and children all worked long hours every day (save a part of Sunday). They did not choose to double their material income; they chose to forego some of their potential income in order to "purchase" the free time that had been denied them as slaves. In doing so, their work-leisure patterns moved toward those that have been adopted by most other free labor forces. Adolescents, women with children, and elderly blacks virtually ceased to work for hire. Adult men and women who remained in the labor force insisted on portions of Saturday, as well as all Sunday, off.

This change in work effort meant that the man-hours supplied by the rural black population were reduced by 28 to 37 percent per capita.[14] Such a large and dramatic fall in the aggregate supply of labor had a pronounced effect on the newly organized market for free labor. Landowners throughout the South complained of a great "labor shortage." One South Carolina planter summarized the various reasons for this shortage and estimated its impact to have been even greater than we have suggested: Black workers "lose many days, they get to work late, remain longer at meals, and refuse to work on Saturdays after 12. Taking this into consideration and adding the withdrawal of women from the field, and of the very many of the young negroes, boys or girls, who are seldom compelled by their parents to work, we can safely say that since the termination of the war the labor devoted to agriculture at the South has diminished by one half."[15]

With a smaller effective labor supply, less land could be put back into production. A comparison of the 1860 and 1870 censuses suggests that the cultivated acreage in the five cotton states of the South fell by more than 20 percent over the Civil War decade.[16] The agricultural output per capita in the South declined markedly due to the reduced inputs of both labor and land. We have estimated elsewhere that a reduction of approximately 26 percent in per capita output could be attributed to this effect.[17] The fact that output per *person* declined does not imply that the output per *man-hour* (that is to say, labor productivity) fell. Moreover, the decline in output per capita should not be interpreted to suggest that blacks were unable to reap the full economic benefits from emancipation. Contemporary accounts make it clear that the partial withdrawal of labor was a voluntary action by the free blacks, who must have felt that the income foregone was less valuable than the free time it released.[18]

The contraction of the labor supply had an economic implication quite apart from its direct effects on production. In the free market for labor, landowners would have to vigorously compete with each other to hire workers. This turn of events would give blacks a degree of economic power that they might use to their advantage, either to increase their material income or to gain other concessions from the landowners.

Initially, landowners sought to prevent the emergence of a competitive labor market. Planters urged each other to refrain from competitive bidding for labor among themselves. Sidney

Andrews, a journalist touring the South in 1865, reported that in areas of South Carolina a freedman needed to show a "consent paper" from his former owner before he could be hired by a new employer and that in Barnwell County there was a "patrol and pass system" reminiscent of the slave days.[19] Such practices were given legal support when the southern state governments, recognized by President Andrew Johnson in the summer of 1865, enacted legislation that came to be called black codes. These laws were explicitly designed to curb the civil rights of freedmen and particularly to limit their economic freedoms. Although the specifics varied from state to state, the general provisions of the codes were uniform. They forbade prospective employers from offering a higher wage to any freedman already employed. A freedman who violated his contract could be penalized by losing wages, a portion of which had invariably been withheld against just such a possibility. The unemployed ran the risk of being arrested under the vagrancy statutes, which stated that any freedman not gainfully employed was a "vagrant" and subject to fine. Once convicted, the prisoner could be hired out to a local planter—at minimal wages—to pay the fine. So long as such laws remained on the books, they were enforced vigorously, and their effect was to prevent competition from developing in the labor market.

Despite this initial success, the landlords' efforts to control wages and the labor market ultimately failed. Congress in 1866 overturned the black codes, and the military commanders in the South sought to insure that these pernicious laws were not enforced by local authorities. This effectively removed the legal basis for collusion among planters. At the same time, the Freedmen's Bureau, created in 1865, had become organized enough to police the labor market and facilitate the contracting procedure. As John Trowbridge observed in the winter of 1866, "The presence of the Bureau at this time was an incalculable benefit to both parties. It inspired the freedmen with confidence and persuaded them, with the promise of protection, to hire out once more to Southern planters."[20] Trowbridge, to be sure, overlooked the fact that the bureau was not always sensitive to the interests of the blacks. For example, the pressure exerted by bureau agents to "persuade" blacks to sign contracts with planters in some cases undermined the freedmen's attempts to acquire their own land by withholding labor. Still, the bureau saw to it that landowners used a standard contract format, which clearly spelled out the obligations of both parties, and insisted that local landowners offer wages comparable with those offered in nearby regions. Because most landowners had no choice but to work through the bureau, its agents were able to reduce the effectiveness of collusion among employers. By the second season of hiring, competitive scrambling for the scarce laborers had begun, and within another year the balance of economic power had clearly shifted from landlord to laborer.

Once the attempt to prevent the establishment of a competitive labor market failed, the only question that remained was how the blacks would choose to use their newly acquired market influence. Apparently blacks felt that a change in the working conditions was most important, since they immediately requested that the plantation lands be subdivided and rented to them for a share of the crop. Contemporaries emphasized the tenacity of these demands for sharecropping. Blacks would settle for no other system. As one farmer complained in 1868, "A share in the crop is the universal plan; negroes prefer it and I am forced to adopt it."[21] Another landowner confirmed that landowners felt they had no option: "I had to yield, or lose my labor."[22]

The blacks' acquisition and exercise of the freedom to contract in the presence of an acute labor shortage meant that the transition from the work-gang technology of the plantation to tenant farming was sudden and nearly complete. The rise of sharecropping was a direct consequence, therefore, of emancipation. The transformation can be viewed as the outcome of an economic process in which the blacks imposed their preference for tenancy upon landowners at a time when there was no effective resistance. Our reading of the contemporary literature has convinced us that the blacks appreciated the situation. They viewed their struggle with the landowners as primarily economic, they knew they had a degree of economic power, and they knew what their own priorities were. When a Mississippi freedman was warned in 1866 that "the whites intend to compel you to hire out to them," the man replied, "What if we should compel them to lease us lands?"[23]

Why did blacks choose sharecropping?

The scenario just sketched raises the questions of why blacks used their advantage to acquire the right of tenancy, rather than to extract higher wages from a plantation system, and why they chose that particular form of tenancy. In part the desire to become tenant farmers was a reaction against the work-gang system. The former slave's objection to the wage plantation was that it bore too close a resemblance to slavery. Work gangs, slave quarters, overseers, and, in some cases, use of corporal punishment did not seem to constitute the freedom promised by emancipation. To former slaves, freedom could not be complete unless they were free from the day-to-day control of their lives by others. This ideal seemed to require that they become independent farm operators. Blacks would have preferred, of course, to own land outright. But this opportunity was closed to them, if not by their own poverty then by the refusal of whites to sell, or even to rent, small holdings to blacks. As Sidney Andrews observed, "In Beaufort District [South Carolina] they not only refuse to sell land to negroes, but also refuse to rent it to them; and many black men have been told that they would be shot if they leased land and undertook to work for themselves."[24] Whitelaw Reid, another northern traveler, made a similar observation regarding land along the Mississippi River, and the instances of violence against black landholders documented in the congressional hearings provide ample testimony of the extremes that white resistance to landownership by blacks could reach.[25] Quite apart from white hostility, independent farming by blacks was seldom feasible, at least in the immediate postwar period. Mortgage payments or fixed rents would have had to be paid, and the farmer would have had to provide his own workstock and farm capital. Without assets or access to organized credit markets, most blacks could not have secured the necessary funding to operate their own farms. Sharecropping circumvented these difficulties. The landowner provided the necessary working capital.

In these circumstances, blacks saw sharecropping as the most attractive form of land tenure available to them. A move from wage labor to sharecropping not only put each black family on its own farm, but also freed them from the day-to-day control over the minutiae of their work effort by the overseer. To be sure, the owner retained the right to supervise the farm operation in order to protect his own interest in the crop. But such management was confined to the basic economic decisions and did not typically require close, daily overseeing.

Blacks were not the only ones who saw sharecropping as an improvement over the work-gang technology. Throughout the South in 1866 and 1867 there were landlords who had experimented with a variety of tenure arrangements. From these experiments a workable form of sharecropping had emerged. Landowners who had offered tenants a share of the crop frequently found that their returns from this system equaled, and in some cases exceeded, those obtainable with the plantation system. Although some whites continued to oppose sharecropping because it accorded blacks more personal freedom than whites would have liked, most landlords put their economic interest ahead of their prejudice and agreed to subdivide their land into tenancies. Sharecropping became a permanent feature of the southern countryside. The new system worked because the motivating force of the overseer and slave driver had been replaced by the less obvious, but equally effective, incentive provided by the workers' own interest in maximizing productivity per acre. Thus, the landlord could accede to black insistence on more independence without jeopardizing his own income.

Blacks insisted upon sharecropping not only because it afforded them a much greater degree of personal freedom, but because it offered some very tangible incentives as well. Dividing the crop meant that any increase in farm output increased the farmer's income as well as the landlord's. Such a reward, whether it resulted from extra effort or from good fortune, would not be shared with labor paid a fixed wage. This fact took on great importance in the early postwar years because of the planters' inexperience in dealing with hired labor. Conditioned by their experience with slave labor, most whites had a low opinion of blacks' potential as free laborers. As a result, they initially offered wages that were quite low. Their prediction of low productivity became, in part, self-fulfilling. Workers paid a low wage had little incentive to put forward their best effort, and whites saw the poor performance as justification for maintaining the wage. Black workers, in these circumstances, knew that output would be increased if they were offered an appropriate incentive to produce it. As a result, sharecropping attracted workers with its potential for higher income as well as its more favorable working conditions.

This is a point worth emphasizing, for sharecropping is frequently identified as an exploitative system of land tenure. Our analysis suggests this is not so. Sharecropping attracted black workers because it offered them greater rewards than wage labor. We see no evidence in our analysis of the returns to various forms of tenure that black sharecroppers received less income than other farm families. Returns to cash renters and sharecroppers seem to be virtually identical,[26] and the wage rates that prevailed generally in the South at this time for hired laborers suggest it is unlikely that wage earners would have a material income above that of tenants.[27] If there was exploitation of labor in southern agriculture after the war, it did not depend upon the form of labor contract agreed to by the two contracting parties.[28]

What was sharecropping's contribution to economic growth?
Although we are confident that sharecropping was adopted largely at the insistence of blacks and certainly not as a substitute for slavery, we cannot be so sanguine about its long-term economic consequences. Sharecropping was an integral part of an agricultural system that, for the last forty years of the nineteenth century, failed to keep pace with the growth and development of the American economy. Between 1871 and 1904 in the South, the gross crop output per capita increased annually by only 1.17 percent. The United States' economy as a whole, by contrast, grew at an annual rate of 2.74 percent over that period.[29] Both this relatively slow rate of growth and the inability of the South to move resources from farming to a more productive sector reflect the fact that southern agriculture was confronted with a system that stymied development by limiting opportunities for investment, curtailing migration, and concentrating production on a single cash crop. Sharecropping contributed to this outcome by weakening the economic incentives to investment in agriculture.

Dividing each year's crop between laborer and landowner reduced the landlord's incentive to invest in the tenant's farm because he would receive only one-half the increase in output attributable to the capital improvement. In effect, the capital investment contemplated would have to yield twice the normal return before the landlord would be willing to finance it. The tenant would be reluctant to contribute toward any capital improvement since his direct interest in the land was limited to the current year. Because most of the potential investments would yield their return over many years, the tenant would share in only a small fraction of the gains unless he was guaranteed security of tenure. However, division of the output necessitated short-term contracts. The laborer, though he enjoyed some incentive for extra effort from the sharing arrangement, would never be able to recoup the full benefit from his marginal effort. As a result, landlords were confronted with a persistent problem of ensuring that the tenant family applied sufficient labor to cultivate his rented land intensively enough. Labor obligations could be (and were) written into the sharecropping contract, but such "guarantees" could only be directly enforced with difficulty. Annual contracting and insecurity of tenure allowed a regular review of performance, so that a family that failed to adequately meet its labor obligation could be refused the right to re-contract for the coming season.[30]

As a result, the cropper saw little advantage in contributing to the improvement of the farm when there was only an uncertain possibility of reaping the benefits beyond the current year. Southern landowners recognized that they were, in general, fortunate if they were able to merely enforce the provisions for farm maintenance that were written into the standard contract. As a Tennessee farmer noted, sharecroppers "will not make a rail or a board, or clean off a ditch or do anything to keep up the place, unless they are paid extra."[31]

Only in the special case when the entire return from a given investment was earned within a single crop year could the sharing of investment expenses be justified. The only important investment expenditure of this type in southern agriculture was fertilizer, the effect of which primarily was to increase crop yields in the current year. Sharecroppers frequently arranged to share the fertilizer cost with the landowner, and fertilizer was used extensively to improve crop yields in the South. But short-term investments of this nature could not lead to sustained growth in agricultural productivity. In the long run, their main impact was to forestall the decline in crop yields that would have resulted from soil exhaustion in the absence of fertilizer.

Did sharecropping serve the ends of race control?
Sharecropping was primarily an economic institution, established in a market context to facilitate agricultural production. Nevertheless, it would be rare to find a purely economic institution; indeed, most of society's institutions serve multiple ends. At the very least, economic institutions must be compatible with the broader objectives of the society of which they are a part. It is well known that southern society of the late nineteenth century was one in which power was almost exclusively in the hands of whites. They controlled the political process, they shaped the educational and social institutions of the South to serve their own ends, and they owned the bulk of the means of production. It is also well known that racism was not extinguished with the abolition of slavery. Indeed, a major objective of the white elite in the postwar period was to perpetuate some sort of inferior status for the former slave. The maintenance of white supremacy required not only that blacks have an inferior political position and fewer civil liberties; it also required that blacks be placed in an inferior economic position, in the sense of both a lower material standard of living and a lower standing in the economic hierarchy.

When considering the role of sharecropping in furthering the ends of white supremacy, it is important to distinguish between the forces that led to the emergence of sharecropping and the reasons the institution proved compatible with southern society. As we have seen, it cannot be argued that sharecropping was imposed by whites on an unwilling but powerless black population. Instead, it is closer to the truth to say that sharecropping was imposed by blacks on a reluctant class of white landowners.

This is not to suggest that white supremacy and the strong pressure to maintain control over blacks did not influence the reorganization of agricultural production. Whites turned to legal and extralegal compulsion to prevent the freedmen from becoming landowners themselves, thus compelling blacks to accept something less than proprietorship. This may be an academic point, for in the late 1860s few blacks had the means to purchase land. But, as the balance of the century unfolded, the barriers to Negro landownership were used to hold blacks in an economic status that whites viewed as inferior. If it is not surprising to learn that the black majority of the cotton South owned only 6.7 percent of the farmland in 1880, it should be disturbing to discover that the 1900 census reported that blacks owned only 6.5 percent of the farmland in the five major cotton states.[32]

If whites truly felt that they were forced to yield to blacks who insisted on sharecropping contracts rather than accept wage payments, they soon found that the new system did not threaten either their social or their economic position. As we have suggested, whites found that economic returns from their tenant farms were quite satisfactory. Just as important, the cropper did not succeed in elevating himself to the status of an equal partner; it was the landlord who made the important economic decisions and supervised the labor and who could dismiss the tenants when they proved unsatisfactory. Although white control had been significantly reduced, the white landowner was still clearly the dominant partner.

The landowners' superior position in the economic hierarchy was paralleled by their higher standard of living. Despite the fact that slave owners were not compensated when abolition deprived them of their slaves and that they thereby experienced a substantial reduction in their net worth, they nevertheless emerged from the war with considerably more assets than their former bondsmen did. They were set free without property of any kind. The standard of living that blacks could earn as laborers was still far below that of whites with property income.

Although probably not designed to do so, sharecropping helped to perpetuate the marked disparity in material well-being between the landowner and his workers. The discouragement to investment inherent in sharecropping slowed the pace of economic development and retarded the adoption of new techniques that might have raised agricultural productivity. Moreover, a stagnant southern agriculture was not an environment conducive to black advancement. Without economic growth, black advances could come only at the expense of some other group, and blacks were hardly in a political position to effect a redistribution of income or wealth. Nor were the institutional arrangements inherent in sharecropping particularly conducive to economic self-advancement. The tenant farmer had little opportunity to learn the intricacies of marketing and finance, since the landowner or the merchant performed these functions. The institution did not prove to be the first step on an agricultural ladder to eventual landownership for blacks.

The slow economic progress of southern agriculture meant that tenant farmers remained poor throughout the last half of the nineteenth century, and poverty itself effectively held the black in his inferior place. He could afford to save little of his income, and thus could neither educate his children nor invest time and money in acquiring more productive skills on his own. Poverty also effectively ruled out the possibility of leaving southern agriculture for higher-paying jobs in urban areas or the North. Not until the early decades of this century did a combination of external forces allow a Negro exodus from the South.

Viewed strictly as a problem in economic theory, the analysis of southern sharecropping seems to lead to the conclusions that sharecropping arose in response to market forces, did not lend itself to the exploitation of black labor, achieved a level of economic efficiency comparable with that of alternative arrangements, and could be faulted primarily only because it reduced the rate of investment. It is true that such conclusions do not support an assertion that sharecropping was a mechanism of social control, but, on the other hand, they do not support an assertion that it could *not* have served such a purpose. Historical questions of this kind can be meaningfully analyzed only from a broader perspective. Historians, of course, have provided just such a broad perspective, but their analysis can sometimes be faulted for oversimplifying an inherently complex process. It would be a mistake to argue that, because sharecropping was compatible with the racist goals of the white elite, it was therefore inefficient, exploitative, or instituted as a substitute for slavery. In short, sharecropping was both a market response *and* a mechanism of race control.

After Emancipation:

A Comparative Study of White Responses to the New Order of Race Relations in the American South, Jamaica & the Cape Colony of South Africa

GEORGE M. FREDRICKSON

Thirty years have passed since Frank Tannenbaum published the little book that opened up the study of comparative slavery and race relations in the Americas. He called it *Slave and Citizen* to show that his subject was not merely patterns of servitude but also incompassed what happened after emancipation. The extent to which freedmen gained citizenship rights or were otherwise encorporated into the societies in which they found themselves was, if anything, more important to him than how they had fared under slavery.[1] But subsequent historians, who either built on Tannenbaum's work or reacted against it, have generally been much more concerned with the slave than with the citizen. Comparative slavery has become a flourishing enterprise, but the postemancipation responses and adjustments of those who had formerly been masters and slaves remain relatively undeveloped as subjects for cross-cultural historical study. This narrowing of concern may have promoted a clearer perception of slave systems, but it has also limited our ability to understand the forces involved in the transformation from a racial order based on black slavery to a more ambiguous situation, where formal affirmations of freedom and equality clashed with the desire of many whites to institute new forms of racial oppression.

If Tannenbaum's successors have neglected to pursue his interest in the aftermath of slavery, they may have followed him too closely in restricting their comparisons to New World societies. There were in fact colonial slave regimes in the Eastern Hemisphere as well as the Western. Yet there has been no effort by historians to shed light on developments in the United States or other parts of the New World by considering what occurred in places like the Cape Colony of South Africa or the important sugar island of Mauritius in the Indian Ocean.[2] Including new and hitherto unfamiliar cases in our comparative frame of reference might significantly aid our understanding of the processes involved in racial stratification.

One way to further the comparative study of postemancipation race relations, and at the same time enlarge the scope of our geographical awareness, would be to compare local white response to the freeing of slaves and the abolition of legal and political distinctions based on race or color in three areas where this dual process occurred in a relatively sudden, concentrated, and formalized fashion in the middle decades of the nineteenth century—the southern United States, the Cape Colony of South Africa, and Jamaica. In the slave societies of Latin America, the actual emancipation process was actually largely completed through manumission before the formal abolition of slavery; and the legalized racial distinctions of the colonial era, the system of *castas,* had already crumbled by the early nineteenth century under the weight of extensive miscegenation and the demands of prolonged independence struggles.[3] But in the South, the Cape Colony, and Jamaica, whites had to rapidly adjust both to the abolition of slave systems that had shown few signs of eroding away and to the almost simultaneous implementation of a doctrine of legal and political equality that ran counter to local traditions. Hence, they faced a challenge that has no real analogue in the history of Iberian America. By limiting our attention to three multiracial societies of northwest European origin that experienced similar emancipations, we simplify the process of comparative analysis—and perhaps make it more meaningful—by avoiding the kind of gross differences not only in the character of emancipation, but also in cultural and religious traditions, that complicate all comparisons with Latin America. We thus narrow to more manageable size the number of factors that have to be taken into account, and we can devote greater attention to situational or environmental conditions, as opposed to the less tangible realm of inherited cultural values and attitudes.

Since it is an accepted rule of thumb for comparative study that the greater the similarities the more significant the differences, it is important at the outset to chart the common ground. In all three of our instances the new order was imposed from without on an unwilling or at least reluctant white population; the role played by the North in forcing emancipation and Reconstruction on the southern states in the 1860s was played by the British government in both Jamaica and South Africa during the 1830s. As we have seen, the new order involved not merely the abolition of slavery as a legal status but also efforts to place emancipated slaves and other free people of color on a footing of civil and political equality with whites. The South, the Cape, and Jamaica in fact constitute the three principal examples of former slave societies where freedmen and other people of color were, for a time, granted voting rights on the same basis as whites and, to varying degrees, actually exercised those rights within a framework of representative government. But such experiments in civil and political color blindness proved abortive; in all three cases substantive egalitarianism failed to take hold; and white supremacy, in one form or another, was maintained or reestablished.

The common elements in this pattern of development resulted

mainly because all three areas were exposed to similar pressures from the metropole or dominant region. Jamaica and the Cape were of course British colonies, and the defeated South of the Reconstruction era was for a time politically subservient to the victorious North. External ideological currents, as well as the willingness of those in power to act on them, shaped the new order and at least temporarily limited local white initiatives to transform or overthrow it.

The most pervasive ideological development affecting these slave societies was the growth in Great Britain and the northern United States of a powerful commitment to free-labor capitalism. This orientation inevitably encouraged a harsh appraisal of local systems of involuntary labor that deviated from the recently sanctified norms of the mother country or dominant section. Once the labor systems of the South, the Cape, or Jamaica were popularly acknowledged in the metropole to be antithetical to capitalistic conceptions of economic progress, the stage was set for the fusion of economic liberalism with another strong intellectual tendency—the philanthropic impulse spawned by the evangelical revivals of the late eighteenth and early nineteenth centuries.

The humanitarian crusade, of which the antislavery movement became a central component, drew its emotional force from the spiritual egalitarianism of the revivals and from a new stress on active "benevolence" in the form of sympathetic action to uplift the downtrodden and convert the unconverted. But, as David Brion Davis suggests in his analysis of the early antislavery movement in England, the humanitarians were also exponents par excellence of emerging bourgeois values, and their ideological lenses tended to filter out the near-at-hand sufferings occasioned by capitalistic development, while clearly reflecting the agonies of slaves or aborigines farther from home. They therefore may have played a major part in giving legitimacy to a rising capitalistic order by contrasting its idealized image with a picture of slave or colonial society as the scene of unmitigated cruelty, barbarism, and immorality.[4]

If Davis's interpretation is correct and if it can be extended both ahead in time and across the Atlantic, it would help explain the momentum that the antislavery movement was able to generate in the American North and the ease with which religious humanitarianism and capitalistic economic attitudes could come together to form an effective antislavery consensus. For northern Republicans of the 1850s, as for British colonial reformers and their evangelical supporters in the 1830s, the slaveholding section may have served as a powerfully evocative "contrast conception," indispensable for validating or legitimating a new order at home.[5]

When the metropolitan free-labor ideology became politically or militarily overpowering, the dominant whites in our three societies were not only forced to abandon slavery but also to eliminate civil and political distinctions based on race or color that had been a by-product of racial servitude. The ultimate failure to achieve the egalitarian promise of the new order was due partly to a decline in the humanitarian component in the capitalistic ideology of the metropole. The waning of humanitarianism, beginning in England in the 1850s and 1860s and in the United States in the 1860s and 1870s, and its eventual replacement by a "tough-minded" racial and social Darwinism, involved a complex process of the popularization of pseudoscientific racism and hereditarianism, a hard-boiled new attitude toward lower-class suffering as the price of progress and the "survival of the fittest," and a widespread disenchantment with the trouble and expense of uplifting "lesser breeds."[6] Whatever the cause of this shift in attitudes, it provided new opportunities to those whites in the South, Jamaica, and the Cape who wished to modify or subvert the new order. The external pressure was either eased or took a new form, and the persisting inequalities in local power and prestige were allowed to solidify, thus thwarting the revolutionary potential of the new order, and white supremacy achieved a new coherence and stability that would prove hardy and long lasting.

The reaction of local whites to the ideological and political pressures exerted by the metropole and its representatives was inspired in each case by the desire to keep as many of their old privileges as possible. Yet, the nature and outcome of the whites' struggle to guarantee their dominance by means other than slavery varied significantly in the three societies. If white supremacy was the common goal, the means used to achieve it and the forms through which white power operated were surprisingly diverse. In fact, a comparative sociologist searching for a typology for differentiating postemancipation white-supremacist regimes might find here almost a full range of the possible modes of white domination.

In the American South, to make a long story short, white supremacists vigorously resisted the new order and employed a combination of terror and political mobilization to reestablish rule by a white elite in the 1870s. After about twenty years of maintaining racial subordination by informal pressures and comparatively subtle legal devices, the ruling group resorted in the 1890s and thereafter to legalized segregation and disfranchisement, partly because of new challenges to their hegemony by dissident whites, who were sometimes willing to make political alliances with blacks, and partly because of the unlikelihood of renewed federal intervention in behalf of black equality in the South.[7] The result by 1910 was an elaborately formalized pattern of caste domination, operating under the constitutional cover of "separate but equal" and a qualified franchise, but which in fact assigned flagrantly unequal facilities to blacks and systematically manipulated the voting restrictions to eliminate the black electorate.

In Jamaica, the white colonists tried to adapt to the new order and turn it to their advantage. But their attempts to establish a plantocracy based on free labor and formal equality were seriously hampered by an economic and demographic decline, which had begun under slavery but was greatly exacerbated in the 1840s by the triumph of free trade in England. The fall in the number and prosperity of the white planters and the rise of an independent black peasantry that seemed destined to take power help account for the panic of white Jamaica after a local black uprising in 1865. In the wake of the Morant Bay rebellion, the island's Assembly voted itself out of existence and accepted direct rule by the British crown.[8] The period of crown colony administration beginning in 1866 gave to local whites insurance against black domination. The unique solution of the Jamaicans was to place their society under a form of imperial rule designed primarily for colonies composed overwhelmingly of "natives," who allegedly required indefinite guardianship and supervision. In effect they induced the British government—in an era when it was increasingly influenced by the view that Negroes were congenital savages to be ruled with an iron hand—to assume the "white man's burden," thereby relieving themselves of an apparently hopeless task.[9]

The South African response was more complex and in fact involved two disparate solutions to the problem of maintaining white supremacy under the new order. The emancipation of slaves and the liberation of a substantial population of detribalized indigenes from a system of compulsory labor resembling serfdom impelled a portion of the white population to leave the colony and establish independent republics where racial inequality was constitutionally sanctioned and de facto African enslavement, under the guise of "apprenticeship," was widely practiced.[10] A larger segment of the white population remained within the colony and pragmatically adjusted to the new order. In contrast to the Jamaicans, they succeeded in the decades after emancipation in gaining a *greater* measure of self-government; the Cape in fact gained a high degree of local autonomy about the time Jamaica was losing hers and did so without abandoning the principle of legal and political equality associated with emancipation. The franchise established in the Cape when representative government was granted in 1854 was formally color-blind, and no specifically racial distinctions were enacted into law by the new parliament. There were no legal sanctions for segregation or even against miscegenation. Yet a racial hierarchy clearly existed in society if not in law. Although some nonwhites voted, only whites were actually elected to parliament. Whites effectively controlled the economic system and commanded the labor of nonwhites on their own terms.[11] If the South and the Boer republics instituted or reestablished a legalized racial caste system and if white Jamaica accepted imperial guardianship to ossify the status quo, the Cape colonists held the reins of racial power by an astute application of the conventional devices of class rule.

To get a better sense of these differing outcomes, it is useful to imagine a hypothetical traveler visiting the South, Jamaica, and the Cape around the turn of the century. In Dixie he would have seen Jim Crow in full flower with "separate and unequal" dominating all aspects of life. In Jamaica he would have found little overt public discrimination; he would have noticed, however, that almost all power was in the hands of an imperial bureaucracy that showed some paternalistic concern for black welfare but a much greater devotion to the interests of white capital. In Cape Town he would have encountered white politicians appealing to nonwhite voters and an atmosphere of racial fluidity and public mixing, which might have made him wonder if he had taken the wrong ship and ended up in Brazil by mistake.[12] To begin to understand and explain these differing white reactions to the new order and the divergent modes of white supremacy that finally crystallized, we must look more closely first at the contrasting ecological and social settings in which these developments took place and then at differences in the political and ideological circumstances under which the new orders were instituted.

Jamaica was of course a prime example of a tropical exploitation colony. By the time the British took possession from the Spanish in 1655, the indigenous population of Arawak Indians had been exterminated, and slaves were imported from Africa to work on the sugar plantations that soon became the mainspring of the island's economy. Besides the relatively level plantation areas where most of the slaves were concentrated, Jamaica had an extensive and ruggedly mountainous backcountry, which served as a haven for maroons and runaways. By the end of the seventeenth century the local whites were greatly outnumbered by the imported slaves. Throughout the eighteenth century the ratio held firm at about ten to one, and by the time of emancipation in 1834 the gap had widened.[13] Since most white settlers were unattached males, open concubinage with slave women became not only common but socially acceptable. Edward Long, the first historian of Jamaica, noted in the 1770s that "he who should presume to show any displeasure against such a thing as simple fornication would for his pains be accounted a simple blockhead; since not one in twenty can be persuaded that there is either sin or shame in cohabiting with a slave."[14] These liaisons resulted in the growth of a substantial free-colored class, which by the time of emancipation probably outnumbered the whites by about two to one.[15] This important mulatto group served as an intermediate caste during slavery and in general identified more closely with the whites than with the black slaves. During the emancipation era its spokesmen fought with some success for inclusion within the ruling class.[16]

The shrinking population of whites still on the island at the time of abolition did not include the actual owners of most of the plantations. Philip Curtin has estimated that two-thirds or more of the estates under cultivation were owned by absentees residing in England.[17] The influential local whites tended to be agents or managers supervising the plantations of absentees, although most of them owned some land of their own as well.[18] Lower down the social scale were the nonelite whites, the majority of whom were directly dependent on the managerial plantocracy as subordinate supervisory personnel, as "sufficiency men" kept on the plantations mainly as a security measure under laws designed to decrease the likelihood of slave rebellions, and as "jobbers," the small slaveholders whose income was largely derived from hiring out their slaves as supplementary labor for the plantations during busy seasons.[19]

The foremost concern of the local plantocracy was economic survival. Committed to plantation agriculture mainly as a means of gaining enough wealth to return to England as absentee proprietors, they tended to view emancipation in terms of how it affected their dreams of success. Jamaica had been declining economically since the Napoleonic wars, and abolition seemed likely to deliver the *coup de grâce* unless the former slaves could be induced to continue working on the plantations at low wages. Emancipation was therefore viewed primarily as a labor problem, and efforts to solve it were greatly hindered by the existence of an extensive backcountry unsuitable for sugar cultivation but well adapted to semisubsistence farming. Hence, many of the freedmen had the option of deserting the plantations and becoming peasant proprietors, a choice unavailable in most other plantation societies after emancipation.[20]

Unlike Jamaica, the Cape was a colony of permanent settlement with a healthy temperate climate. An outpost of the Dutch East India Company until taken over by the British—temporarily from 1795 to 1803 and permanently in 1806—it was, comparatively speaking, an economic failure and would remain so until the discovery of diamonds and gold in southern Africa in the 1870s and 1880s. Because of the aridity of all but a small fraction of the territory acquired by the company before the 1830s, the agricultural potential was extremely limited. In contrast to

Jamaica and the American South, the colony produced no important staples for export during the slave era, and consequently no real plantation system developed.[21] Lack of economic opportunity kept the white population small and widely dispersed; in 1820 there were only forty thousand whites spread out over a vast territory. The whites at this time were outnumbered by the nonwhites in the colony but not by anything like the proportion that existed in Jamaica or that would exist later in South African history. The nonwhites within the borders of the colony comprised thirty thousand imported slaves and about the same number of so-called Hottentots, the largely detribalized descendants of the region's aborigines. Hence, the ratio of nonwhite to white was about one and a half to one, demographically similar to portions of the lower South in the same period.[22] Later in the century the population ratio would change drastically after incorporation into the colony of extensive territories inhabited by Bantu-speaking Africans.

Slavery had been introduced by the Dutch East India Company in the seventeenth century because of a shortage of white labor and the alleged unsuitability of the nomadic Hottentots for sedentary occupations. A substantial proportion of the slaves were East Indians transported from the company's Asian possessions, but a majority seems to have been black Africans imported from Mozambique and Madagascar.[23] Throughout the era of slavery most of them worked as laborers on the wine and grain farms of the limited fertile region of the western Cape or in urban occupations in Cape Town itself. By the middle decades of the eighteenth century, the indigenous Hottentots had been deprived of their cattle and grazing land and were being incorporated into the colonial economy as pastoral serfs, a development reflecting the growth of grazing as a frontier occupation and a basis for rapid white expansion into the semiarid regions to the east and north of the original settlement.[24]

As in Jamaica, the shortage of white females led to extensive race mixture in the seventeeth and eighteenth centuries. But unlike Jamaica, concubinage was not the only acceptable form of interracial union. To a surprising extent Dutch males took women of color as legal spouses and succeeded in having their offspring accepted as part of the white burgher community.[25] But those of mixed origin who were not the products of legal unions or who were simply too dark to be acceped by white society were relegated to a free-colored class, which became the object of increasing racial discrimination by the late eighteenth century.[26] Eventually the free people of color, the emancipated slaves, and the surviving Hottentots would merge to form the Cape Coloreds. But the line between light coloreds and whites would remain vague and permeable. Until recently—some would say up to the present day—"passing for white" was a significant social and even demographic phenomenon in the western Cape.[27]

At the time of emancipation the Bantu-speaking Africans, who now constitute the overwhelming majority of the South African population, were considered an independent people beyond the borders of the colony, although a series of frontier wars reflected a lack of agreement on where the borders actually were. Within the colony, therefore, the various colored groups, which were beginning to coalesce into a conglomerate population of multi-racial origins, did not constitute a relatively privileged inter-mediate category like the Jamaican mulattoes, but in fact formed the lowest class within the society. The difficulty posed for the settlers by the abolition of slavery and the emancipation of the Hottentots from restrictions on their economic freedom was largely a straightforward labor problem like Jamaica's, in-volving a similar search for devices short of slavery or serfdom to force the freedmen to return to their former occupations as agricultural laborers. But the freed people in the Cape lacked the Jamaican option of becoming independent peasants, because there was no land in the colony available for small-scale agri-culture, and even the semiarid pastoral areas were divided up into large, white-owned holdings. The only alternatives to going back to work for white masters were to emigrate from the colony or take refuge on overcrowded mission stations. Despite the loud complaints of white farmers about "vagrancy," there appears to have been less economic disruption because of emancipation than in Jamaica.[28]

One segment of the white population, however, felt particularly aggrieved by emancipation. The seminomadic frontier graziers or trekboers possessed relatively few slaves, but those they did own represented a major share of their limited wealth. Furthermore, they relied heavily on bonded Hottentots as herdsmen and servants. Accustomed to living in isolated frontier conditions that exposed them to the depredations of various indigenous groups, they had acquired a deserved reputation for treating their nonwhite dependents harshly. A long struggle with British humanitarian influences, experienced locally in the form of missionaries who complained to the authorities about how they treated their slaves and servants, had intensified their racial consciousness. Fighting to preserve a white Christian identity in the midst of black and brown heathens, whom they commonly described as *skepsels* (creatures) or progeny of Ham, they were enraged by any threat to their somewhat precarious racial dominance. Such attitudes were why many of them decided to join the Great Trek. It allowed them to opt out of the new racial order by migrating into the interior, where they were free to institutionalize their uncompromising racism.[29]

The physical, economic, and social setting for emancipation and its aftermath in the American South combined certain features reminiscent of the Jamaican or South African situations with some important elements of genuine uniqueness. The Old South had a plantation economy, but most slaveholders were not planters. The forty-six thousand whites who had more than twenty slaves in 1860 may have resembled the plantocracy of Jamaica, but the 88 percent of all slaveholders owning less than

twenty and the 72 percent owning less than ten were comparable in their scale of operations with the general run of masters
of slaves and bonded servants in the Cape. In addition, 75 percent of the white population, mostly small farmers, owned no
slaves at all.[30] Hence the South, like the Cape, had a substantial
class of nonelite slaveholders and was unique in having a white
majority with no direct economic connection with nonwhite
servitude. The overall ratio of white to black was also excep-
tional, since this is the only one of our three cases in which
whites actually outnumbered nonwhites—almost two to one in
all the slave states in 1860.[31]

Like South Africa and unlike Jamaica, the colonial South had
developed as an area of permanent white settlement where
absenteeism was rare. But like Jamaica and unlike South Africa,
its economy from the earliest times was dependent on raising
staples for an external market. Its pattern of geographical expansion recalls the Cape rather than insular Jamaica; but, if the
extension of white settlement in South Africa led to the growth
of a new economy based on livestock raising rather than agriculture, the rise of the southwestern cotton kingdom of the nineteenth century replicated the plantation-based economic system
that had arisen earlier on the eastern seaboard.

Race relations in the preemancipation era took on a character
distinguishable from that of the other two societies. Except to
a limited and precarious extent in some parts of the lower South,
no intermediate mulatto caste developed as in Jamaica.[32] Cape
society may also have evolved toward a two-category system in
the nineteenth century, but in the South the line between the
racial groups was more rigidly drawn and less permeable. Although "passing" occurred, available evidence suggests that it
never did so on the scale and in the almost institutionalized way
characteristic of the Cape Colony. Explaining adequately these
differences in fundamental race patterns would require another
essay as long as this one. But clearly important were the com-

paratively early balancing of the white sex ratio and the presence of a substantial class of nonelite whites, who could perform functions elsewhere assigned to mixed groups. Furthermore, these lower-class whites developed a caste pride that encouraged strict adherence to a "descent rule" under which whiteness was defined in terms of ancestry rather than appearance or culture.[33]

As elsewhere, emancipation created a serious labor problem for former slaveholders. It was eventually resolved primarily through a system of sharecropping that evolved into a veiled form of peonage; for the Afro-American freedmen, like the emancipated coloreds of the Cape, were denied access to land of their own. Once Radical proposals for land confiscation had been rejected, blacks had no alternative but to enter into labor contracts with white planters under arrangements that became increasingly coercive as time went on. Not only was the good land in the plantation districts owned by whites, but the marginal land of the hill country and mountainous areas was, in contrast to Jamaica, already occupied by white farmers. Furthermore, blacks were sometimes inhibited from acquiring land by the terroristic tactics of white vigilante groups.[34]

Yet the reaction of southern whites to the new racial order seems on the whole to have been less affected by purely economic concerns than that of the white Jamaicans or the majority of the Cape colonists. Emancipation presented itself to most southern whites preeminently as a racial or social challenge— a threat to the elaborate structure of caste privilege that had developed before the Civil War. In this they may have resembled the frontier Boers of South Africa, but unlike the dissident Afrikaners they had neither the inclination nor the opportunity to trek away. They had already tried their own mode of secession and had seen their efforts thwarted by the armies of Grant and Sherman.

The differing local settings in which white adaptation to the new order took place did not by itself predetermine the ultimate form of postemancipation race relations. It was rather the interplay of these local conditions with the political and ideological circumstances surrounding the attempted establishment of a new order by external authority that accounts for the divergent varieties of white supremacy that emerged.

In both Jamaica and the Cape Colony, the end of slavery came in the wake of a series of earlier measures to ameliorate slave conditions and improve the status of free people of color. In both areas virtual equality under the law for nonwhites who were not chattel slaves had been legislated before the abolition of slavery—in 1828 in the Cape and in 1830 in Jamaica.[35] As colonial subjects of Great Britain, the local whites in both societies were vulnerable to pressure from the metropole in the 1820s and 1830s in a way that citizens of the "sovereign states" of the American South clearly were not in the 1850s. There was of course some resistance in both colonies to the campaign for humanitarian reform emanating from the Colonial Office and the philanthropic lobby in England. The Jamaican Assembly protested, delayed, and equivocated when called upon by the imperial government to improve the lot of slaves and free people of color. The most conspicuous local agents of British philanthropy, the Baptist missionaries led by the Reverend William Knibb, were threatened by mob violence and temporarily imprisoned after a slave rebellion in 1832; many of their chapels were subsequently burned by angry whites.[36] In the Cape, where there were as yet no representative institutions to give vent to grievances of the white settlers, resistance took the form of petitions, protest meetings, and, at least once, mob action to enforce a boycott of new regulations requiring masters to make regular reports of the punishments given to their slaves.[37] But in neither colony did abolition itself result in serious acts of resistance. Indeed, emancipation seems to have come as something of a relief after the difficulties associated with melioristic interference with the master-slave relationship. Furthermore, the British emancipators sweetened an otherwise bitter pill by providing partial compensation and a period of apprenticeship. Although the latter was designed to ease the transition to freedom, it in fact simply gave the masters four more years of slave labor.[38]

The Great Trek can of course be seen as a dramatic act of resistance to the new order, but it was occasioned less by the abolition of slavery per se than by revulsion at the broader implications of the humanitarian policy. Also, the trekkers were a minority, even of the Dutch-speaking population, and were to some extent following a long-established pattern of frontier expansion, which was deflected in a new direction in the mid-1830s by the British government's refusal to conquer and displace the thickly settled African tribesmen on the eastern frontier.[39]

A major postemancipation issue in both Jamaica and the Cape Colony, as in the United States, was the role of freedmen and other people of color in existing or proposed institutions of local self-government. In Jamaica, abolition automatically conferred the suffrage on former slaves who could meet a property qualification. But even the relatively low property requirement kept the mass of former slaves away from the polls, and a high qualification for office holding limited membership in the Assembly to the economic elite. But propertied mulattoes were routinely elected to the Assembly in the postemancipation years; by 1866 twelve of its forty-eight members were men of color.[40] Between the 1830s and the 1850s there was in fact a strong tendency by whites to admit wealthy and prominent mulattoes into the ruling group; some even rose to positions of leadership and responsibility within the local establishment.[41] But only rarely did colored politicians speak for the interests of the black freedmen. When a former slave was actually elected to the Assembly in 1846, he was refused admittance, and the intervention of the British government was required before he could be seated. By this time large numbers of black peasants had acquired enough property to qualify for the suffrage, but no one effectively mobilized them, and most chose not to register.[42] Elite rule, which no longer meant strictly white rule, was therefore not seriously challenged in the 1840s and 1850s, although the growth of a potential black peasant electorate inspired further efforts to restrict the suffrage.[43] But beginning in the middle fifties, a small group of dissidents emerged within the Assembly. Known to their enemies as the "demagogues," they began to articulate a rudimentary Jamaican nationalism premised on the inevitability of black and brown predominance.[44] The rise of such views, accompanied by a continued decline in the white population and a rise in the black landowning peasantry, set the stage for the hysterical and brutal white response to the Morant Bay uprising of 1865 and the subsequent surrender of self-government.[45]

In the Cape the nonwhite franchise had to await the granting of representative government. For a time the colonial authorities resisted settler demands for an elected assembly partly because of seemingly well-founded fears that the white minority would pass laws oppressing the nonwhite majority. When representative government was finally authorized in 1854, it was on the condition that the franchise be nonracial; the only real issue was whether the property qualification would be high or low. An unlikely coalition of English-speaking liberals, concerned with the protection of nonwhites, and of leading Afrikaners, who wished to include their poorer brethren within the franchise, carried the day for a low qualification.[46]

The white colonists voluntarily accepted a political arrangement that gave former slaves and indigenes a potential voice in government not so much from egalitarian conviction as because they saw no threat to their social and political dominance from a color-blind franchise. By the 1850s, the colored classes of the colony were to a great extent locked once again into their traditional roles as farm laborers and servants. Since the relationship between white and nonwhite corresponded so closely to a European-type class division, the settlers found they could exercise effective control without recourse to legalized social discrimination. Technically color-blind master-servant laws giving the upper hand to employers could thus operate in a de facto racist fashion, and those farm laborers who could qualify to vote were under great pressure to support candidates favored by their masters. Furthermore, the franchise qualification was just high enough, given the substantial European population and the propertyless condition of most nonwhites, to ensure that whites remained a firm majority of the electorate.

By the 1880s, however, the low franchise came under increasing criticism, mainly from Afrikaners who had become aware that the British, a minority of the white settlers, were controlling most of the colored and African vote and using it to dominate the responsible parliamentary government that had existed since 1872. The growth of Afrikaner pressure for a larger share of political power coincided with an increase in the nonwhite vote resulting from the annexation of new African territories. Consequently there was a further restriction of the franchise in the late 1880s and early 1890s. But higher qualifications still left enough nonwhites on the rolls to give them a balance of power in several key districts. There were no more efforts to limit the franchise because, after a genuine two-party system developed in the 1890s, each party found that its hold on certain seats depended on African or Cape Colored votes. When the Cape participated in the deliberations that led to the founding of the Union of South Africa in 1910, its representatives defended almost to a man the principle of an impartial franchise with a property and literacy qualification against the northern Afrikaner or republican tradition of universal white manhood suffrage and nonwhite exclusion. The Cape's white leadership, both English and Afrikaner, had become convinced that their system of "equal rights for civilized men" constituted no threat to white supremacy but rather served as a useful "safety valve" for nonwhite discontent. The unsuccessful struggle to maintain and extend the "Cape liberal tradition" against the growing movement for political and social apartheid would constitute one of the major themes of twentieth-century South African history.[47]

The political and ideological circumstances of emancipation and Reconstruction in the American South differed substantially from those in either the Cape or Jamaica. Of most obvious significance was that emancipation came suddenly and without compensation as the result of a bloody civil war, not gradually and with some adjustment to the desires and interests of local whites as in the British colonies. Furthermore, abolition was followed by the unique phenomenon of Radical Reconstruction involving the enfranchisement of the freedmen on the basis of universal manhood suffrage. Such an extension of full citizenship to a mass of propertyless and largely illiterate former slaves was, by nineteenth-century standards, an extraordinarily bold and radical innovation.[48] Black suffrage, accompanied by the disfranchisement of leading Confederates, represented a far more serious threat to white supremacy than any actions of the British government in relation to its former slave colonies. In addition, the black vote made it possible for a northern-based political party—a party whose original rise to power had provoked southern secession and under whose auspices the military conquest of the Confederacy had been carried out—to achieve temporary dominance over the South. A use of the nonwhite vote for white partisan purposes had also occurred in the Cape, where the English-speaking minority created some ethnic hostility by relying on Cape Coloreds and Africans to outvote the Afrikaner majority. But the nonwhite vote was a relatively small addition to a substantial English settler electorate, not the major source of English political power as the blacks were for the Republicans in many parts of the Reconstruction South. The immense challenge to traditional white prerogatives and concepts of local self-determination that Radical Reconstruction, with all its limitations and deficiencies, actually represented can only be fully appreciated by comparison. From this perspective the currently fashionable assertion that Radical Reconstruction was "not radical enough" seems blatantly ahistorical, although it does call attention to the massive application of force that would have been required to complete the revolution that the Radicals initiated.

The intense and often violent white counterattack to Reconstruction stemmed not only from the magnitude of the provocation but also from the particularly strong racist tradition inherited from the antebellum period. The Herrenvolk ideology, as well as the racial fears that sustained it, had enabled the planter elite to line up most of the nonslaveholding whites behind a system of black servitude that offered them no economic benefits.[49] As we have seen, nonelite whites in Jamaica tended to be directly involved in the plantation economy; those who were no longer needed after emancipation, such as sufficiency men and the slave-renting jobbers, presumably emigrated, helping to account for the continued decline in white population after 1831.[50] In the Cape, on the other hand, those marginal whites most likely to view emancipation and equalization of legal status as a personal affront to their identity as white men tended to join the Great Trek, thereby ceasing to have a direct influence on colonial opinion. But, in the American South, the whites who derived their sense of status from racial pride rather than from real economic and social accomplishment, an element that had always been more significant here than elsewhere, remained in undiminished numbers and served as an apparently inexhaustible source of foot soldiers for collective action in behalf of white supremacy—whether in the form of antiblack rioting, Klan-type terrorism, open paramilitary activity to influence elections, lynching, or the forced removal of blacks from land they owned or rented. The continued need of the dominant group to use control, and accommodate a mass of less-privileged whites helped in complex ways to perpetuate and even strengthen the Herrenvolk tradition in the Reconstruction and post-Reconstruction years. It clearly inhibited the tendency to rely on class rather than race as the formal basis for social and political privilege, which was central to the white ideological response to the new order in both Jamaica and the Cape.[51]

The differences found in 1900 by our mythical traveler would therefore have been primarily due to the contrasting ways in which the new orders had been originally imposed and to the differing ideologies and social situations influencing the local white response. Whether emancipation and formal equality had been perceived as legitimate or at least reconcilable with white attitudes and interests, as generally the case in the British colonies, or as an intolerable imposition to be resisted at almost any cost, as in the South, had turned out to be of lasting significance. Because of peculiarities in the underlying demographic situation, the subjective legacy of the slave era, and the objective circumstances of emancipation and Reconstruction, white southerners had been less able than white Jamaicans or the majority of white settlers in the Cape to make even a limited and pro forma adjustment to color-blind principles of social and political organization. Thus the South went from being a testing ground for the most radical departure from white supremacy attempted anywhere in the nineteenth century to being a blatantly racist order that, in the comprehensiveness of its castelike distinctions, would not be exceeded until the triumph of rigorous apartheid in South Africa after 1948.

The Price of Freedom*

C. VANN WOODWARD

Comparisons are essential to all historical understanding. American understanding of freedom and of the price the nation paid for it has suffered from lack of comparative reference. In proposing such an approach to the study of emancipation and Reconstruction history, I am of course conscious of the recent outburst of interest in the comparative history of slavery and the light it has shed on an American institution that was thereby rendered less peculiar and more understandable. Comparative studies might also help understand what followed slavery. But, though the literature on comparative slavery has reached impressive proportions, very little has been written so far on the comparative history of emancipations and reconstructions. Yet there have been as many emancipations as there have been slavery systems, and we might presume that as much light could be shed upon the American experience by the comparative study of the one as of the other.

The nineteenth century was preeminently the century of emancipations, the period, as Victor Hugo said, of an idea whose

This is a revision of a paper presented at the XIII International Congress of Historical Sciences under the title, "Emancipations & Reconstructions: A Comparative Study," & printed for participants by NAUKA Publishing House, Moscow, 1970.

time had come. Its time came relatively late in the defeated Confederate States of America, for on the world stage more emancipation dramas had been enacted before than after that of 1865. The great age of emancipations was the half-century from 1833, when the British opened it, to 1888, when Brazil (and two years earlier Cuba) belatedly closed it. Earlier small-scale abolitions in the newly independent northern states of British North America were somewhat similar to those of the newly independent states of Spanish South America in that they involved relatively few slaves and in that slavery was comparatively unimportant to their economies. The abolitions and reconstructions of the great age of emancipations were primarily those of plantation America, scattered southward from Virginia to southern Brazil and spread eastward from Texas along the Gulf and through the Caribbean to Barbados. I shall confine this paper to that scope, omitting other areas. This vast area of maritime and continental provinces and nations possessed enough common features and similarities, together with enough differences and cultural variables, to make plantation America, as Charles Wagley says, "a magnificent laboratory for the comparative approach."[1] To explore the opportunities of comparative analysis would require a book. All I can attempt here is to suggest some possibilities and outline the framework of comparison.

Among the common features of the plantation America to which the American South belonged were a one-crop agriculture under the plantation system, a climate suitable for such a system, a background of slavery, a multiracial society, and a large population of African origin. Much more numerous than the common characteristics were the differences that distinguished the component parts. Six imperial powers controlled or had possessed parts of the area—the Spanish, Portuguese, English, French, Dutch, and Danish—not to mention the independent emancipating republics of Haiti, Brazil, and the United States.

These powers were broadly divided in religious traditions between Catholics and Protestants, and their colonies and provinces differed among themselves in the crops they grew, the health and stage of development in their economies, in man-land ratios, and in racial, cultural, and political variables of bewildering complexity. Each of the many emancipations and readjustments involved was a unique historical event, and any valid comparative study will scrupulously respect the integrity of each and avoid facile generalizations. The most natural opportunity for comparison with the experience of the United States, and the one that will most often recur, is that presented by the British West Indies. Most of these colonies shared with the older slave states of the eastern seaboard a history of seventeenth- and eighteenth-century British rule and of populations with similar origins on the black and white sides, together with a common language and many common institutions. Yet, profound differences existed between the society of the island colonies and that of the continental states. Not only that, but probably as many differences existed among the fifteen island colonies that stretched from Jamaica to Trinidad as existed among the fifteen slave states that stretched from Delaware to Texas. The old sugar culture in Barbados, like the old tobacco culture in Virginia, went back to seventeenth-century origins, and, though Guiana and Trinidad were not so new and booming as Louisiana and Mississippi at the time of emancipation, they presented sharp contrasts to the older colonies within the empire. All these differences must be kept in mind when comparisons are ventured.

Since the experience of the United States is central to our concern and its illumination the main purpose of these comparisons, it is well to define first the unique character of its history. In all, some six million slaves were manumitted by the various abolitions of slavery in plantation America between 1834 and 1888. The slave states of the South accounted for four million of them, or about two-thirds of the total. The number liberated in the

South was about five times that on the slave rolls of all the British West Indies in 1834 and eight times that of Brazil in 1888 at the times of abolition. In all the Latin American societies, of course, much liberation preceded abolition. Outside the South the slaves of the British West Indies and Brazil made up the two largest single liberated populations. The emancipation experience of the South therefore dwarfs all others in scale and magnitude.

Another unique feature of the southern experience was the high ratio of whites to blacks. In spite of the enormous number of slaves involved, the white population of the South outnumbered the black two to one. It is true that in two states the freedmen were in the majority and in one approached numerical equality, but nowhere save in isolated spots like the South Carolina Sea Islands did blacks reach such overwhelming preponderance as they did in the Caribbean islands, where ratios reached ten to one, though varying greatly. Three-quarters of the southern whites in 1860 did not belong to slaveholding families, and in them the freedmen faced competition and resistance to their aspirations that they faced nowhere else in plantation America. In all other parts of that great area save Brazil (with many uniquenesses of its own), the dominant cultural tradition was that of a small white minority wielding power over the vast black majority; in the South (and even more in the United States as a whole), the culturally dominant tradition was that of the overwhelming white majority.

Of comparable importance is a third circumstance (among many others) that added vastly to the uniqueness of the South's experience. This was the terrible war that brought about the end of slavery. Wars were not without influence on the weakening of the institution elsewhere, for example in Haiti, Cuba, and Brazil. But nowhere else did a slave society wage a life-and-death struggle for its existence with abolition at stake. And no other war in the western world between those of Napolean and

the two world wars compares with the Civil War in bloodshed
—one life for every six slaves freed and almost as many lives
sacrificed in America as there were slaves liberated in the British
West Indies without any bloodshed. The end of slavery in the
South can be described as the death of a society, though elsewhere it could more reasonably be characterized as the liquida-
tion of an investment. Of the numerous peculiarities that set
apart the South's experience with abolition, then, these three
claim special consideration: the magnitude of emancipation, the
preponderance of whites, and the association with a terrible war.

Neither in Brazil nor in Cuba is the phenomenon of emancipation related to formal abolition in the way emancipation and
abolition are related in the colonies of north European powers—
much less in the American South. In the latter areas the slave
population generally increased in absolute numbers and usually
in proportion to the free population right up to the time of
abolition. Then, after periods of "apprenticeship" or semislavery
(except in the South), all were simultaneously and legally freed.
The situation was strikingly different in Cuba and Brazil. The
slave population in Cuba reached its peak forty-five years, and
in Brazil thirty-eight years, before formal abolition. The number
as well as the proportion of slaves in the total population had
been declining in Cuba since 1841, when there were 421,649
slaves, or a third of the total population. During the 1880s they
dwindled from some 200,000 to fewer than 30,000 before abolition.[2] The slave population of Brazil reached its peak in 1850,
when 2,500,000 constituted about 30 percent of the total population, and before abolition in 1888 the number had declined to
500,000 and the percentage to less than 3.[3]

It is clear that Cuba and Brazil present special problems for
the comparative study of emancipations and reconstructions. The
most elementary and baffling one is to locate these phenomena
in time. It is not a simple choice such as that between 1834 and
1838 as in the case of British emancipation, or between 1863

and 1865 as in the United States. Slavery began to decline in both Cuba and Brazil before the period of abolition laws began, and emancipation had largely run its course before slavery was abolished. In the history of neither of these countries was there any phenomenon like the total emancipation of four millions coinciding with the abolition of slavery that occurred in the American South. Or even the smaller and more gradual process that occurred in the West Indies.

One instance of emancipation remains to be accounted for—one that is an exception to all the others and preceded all the others—that of Haiti, which became the first Negro republic in Western history and the second independent state in the New World. Both emancipation and independence were the products of slave rebellion during the French Revolution, the most successful and the bloodiest slave revolt of modern history. After massacring or driving out all whites, the rulers imposed a tight military control over black labor, dividing all men into laborers or soldiers, making all women laborers, and using the soldiers to impose an iron discipline on workers. With no commitment to tradition and no obligation to foreign white powers, the rulers held a carte blanche for the creation of a new black society and economy. And this is what they created.[4] Emancipation and reconstruction in Haiti involved so many unique circumstances as to make comparisons with its experience of doubtful value.

Statistics on the Atlantic slave trade by Philip D. Curtin illuminate and enrich the comparative study of emancipations and reconstructions. During the whole period of the Atlantic slave trade, legal and illegal, British North America (including Louisiana) received 427,000 or only 4.5 percent of the total imports. This is compared with 4,040,000 or 42.2 percent imported in the Caribbean islands and 3,647,000 or 38.1 percent imported by Brazil.[5] The disparities in imports, especially in view of later slave and Negro populations of the United States and elsewhere, are quite startling.[6] The period of importation is as important for the comparative study of emancipations as the numbers and proportions. For British and North American territory, the legal slave trade ended in 1808. The last years of the trade were the heaviest for many islands, Jamaica importing 63,000 in the last seven years. Illegal trade continued to the United States but added only about 51,000 slaves after 1808. On the other hand, Cuba imported 570,000 between 1808 and 1865. That was 143,000 more than British North America had imported between 1619 and 1860, and it was 80 percent of the total Cuba had imported since the time of Columbus. From 1811 to 1860, Brazil took in 1,145,400 slaves, or nearly a third of its total importation since the sixteenth century and more than three times the number imported by the United States before the legal trade ended in 1808.'

Curtin's statistics add a neglected set of variables to the comparative equation and point up additional aspects of uniqueness in the American experience. The 4,000,000 manumitted American slaves of 1865, as well as the 500,000 free blacks, were descendants of 427,000 Africans. The great majority of them were descended from seventeenth- and eighteenth-century stock (mainly the latter), as are their 20,000,000 or so descendants who are our contemporaries. All but a few were at least two generations removed from their African origins at the time of emancipation, and most of them were more than two generations. They were therefore further removed than any other emancipated population of the New World, and they had been through a longer period of adjustment, accommodation, and acculturation to America and to slavery than any other slave population at the time of abolition. It is true that abolition came a generation later in Cuba and Brazil and that slavery began earlier and lasted longer in both countries. But Cuba imported more than four-fifths of its total in the nineteenth century and, according to Fernando Ortiz, continued to import them up to six years before final abolition. For all of the 3,647,000 slaves landed in Brazil over the centuries, the maximum number of 2,500,000 on the slave rolls at any time was reached in 1850 and declined steadily thereafter. Yet nearly half the latter number were purchased after 1810, and only 500,000 remained on the rolls in 1888.

Of all the numerous components of plantation America, therefore, the American South seems to have had a slave population at the time of abolition that was unique in many respects. Not only was it by far the largest population, but it was derived from the smallest imports in proportion to the number emancipated or to the total black population; it was the furthest removed from African origins; and it had the longest exposure to slave discipline in large numbers. It is difficult to imagine any other slave powers, given the origins and circumstances of their slaves, attempting a simultaneous and total emancipation of their slave populations without periods of apprenticeship or other gradualist devices. At any rate, none of them made the attempt. This is not to suggest that the United States itself was prepared for the bold experiment or that the experiment was a success, but merely that this country was the only one that tried and that, though badly prepared, it was still better prepared in at least some respects than were older countries and colonies.

One of the most distinguished minds ever addressed to the problem of the transition from slavery to freedom was that of Alexis de Tocqueville. In July, 1839, he published a report he made to the French Chamber of Deputies on the abolition of slavery in the French colonies. Tocqueville proposed "an intermediate and transitory state between slavery and liberty," which would serve as "a time of trial, during which the Negroes, already possessing many of the privileges of free men, are still compelled to labor." The transition period he thought to be "indispensable to accustom the planters to the effects of emancipation" and "not less necessary to advance the education of the black population, and to prepare them for liberty." This was, he thought, "the most favorable moment to found that empire over the minds and the habits of the black population." Since Tocqueville believed that "only experience of liberty, liberty long possessed," could prepare a man to be "a citizen of a free country," he thought of the basic issue of reconstruction as a cruel dilemma. In words with universal application for our problem, he wrote "The period which follows the abolition of slavery has therefore always been a time of uneasiness and social difficulty. This is an inevitable evil; we must resolve to meet it, or make slavery eternal." Tocqueville resolved his dilemma with a classic paradox: we must, he declared, "if necessary, compel the laborious and manly habits of liberty."[8] Compelling people to be free raised the ancient problem of reconciling force with freedom, its opposite, and that paradox lay at the heart of the problem of emancipations and reconstructions everywhere in the world.

One precedent for our comparative study is a monograph by a Dutch scholar, Wilhelmina Kloosterboer. In *Involuntary Servitude Since the Abolition of Slavery,* she extends her survey beyond plantation America, to which we are mainly limited, and takes in Africa, Asia, and Oceania. She concludes that some system of involuntary or forced labor almost invariably replaced slavery after abolition in all parts of the world. "Where slavery had been widespread," she writes, "emancipation was followed by the imposition of drastic measures to retain a labour force. Apart from other stipulations there was almost in all cases a decree against 'vagrancy' (Jamaica, Mauritius, South Africa, the United States, the Portuguese Colonies, etc.) which in effect always amounted to compulsory labour when strictly applied." The experience of remote and exotic countries will have a familiar ring to those who know the history of Reconstruction in the South. "The harshness of the measures taken in many countries directly after abolition is not surprising since . . . where the use of Negro slaves was widespread and almost essential for the economy, the direct result of abolition was chaos. The Negroes wanted to get away from their old work on the plantation, for to their minds it was slavery under any name; and the climate in most areas concerned was such as to make it possible for them, at least for a while, to live without having to work at all." Freedmen, under whatever flag and of whatever color, resisted signing labor contracts and sought land for themselves. Forceable measures all had the same purpose: to get the freedmen back to the fields—cotton fields, tobacco fields, sugar fields, coffee fields, all kinds of fields—and mines as well. Whether political control was in the hands of an imperial government or a federal government, it is remarkable how little restraint such authority actually exerted in protecting the lives, civil rights, and human rights of the exploited.[9]

One purpose of this study is to test the validity of this thesis and of Tocqueville's speculations and to see what light they throw on the American experience. When Tocqueville made his report to the Chamber of Deputies in 1839, he had foremost in mind, as he said, "the events which are happening in the British colonies surrounding our own." The previous year the British West Indies had prematurely ended their unhappy experiment with apprenticeship as a sequel to abolition. It had displeased all parties—planters, apprentices, and abolitionists. For all the indulgence, which was beyond the wildest dreams of South Carolina and Mississippi planters who formed the black codes of 1865,[10] the West Indian masters behaved remarkably like their continental cousins thirty years later. Like them the islanders complained when their servants retained the work ethic they had learned as slaves: lying, stealing, malingering, laziness, gross carelessness, and wastefulness. Masters alone knew the Negro character, they declared, and looked back to the old regime for models and techniques of discipline. Given the deferred promise of freedom, great tact was required to get freedmen back to work, but tact was not a part of the average overseer's training. He had been schooled, as the governor of Jamaica remarked, in "the diplomacy of the lash," not in the arts of persuasion.[11]

Colonial legislatures framed black codes that put the later southern state legislatures to shame. Jamaican lawmakers made an undefined crime of "insubordination" punishable by thirty-nine lashes or two weeks on the chain gang and defined "vagrancy" as "threatening" to run away from one's family. A police officer could break up any meeting that he had "reasonable cause" to think would stir up insubordination. On that island an apprentice who absented himself from work for two days in a fortnight was subject to a week on the chain gang or twenty lashes.[12] In legislative initiative and defiance, Jamaica was the Mississippi of the Caribbean on matters concerning Negroes, and other islands often followed its example as closely as they dared. The island legislatures displayed all the ingenuity and determination, for which their southern counterparts later became famous, in subverting the purposes of the abolitionists and recapturing their old powers. In this game of defying the Colonial Office of the home government, the colonial governors were thrust into the unhappy role played by the military governors and carpetbag administrators of the southern states. Complaints of the "sullen intractableness" of West Indian assemblies filed with the Colonial Office would have seemed quite familiar in the Washington, D.C., of the 1860s.[13]

Four years of experience with the apprenticeship system brought it into disrepute in many quarters. Dissatisfaction varied from colony to colony, but it was generally argued that relations between labor and planter had deteriorated and that the system had generated bitter new frictions. Negroes complained endlessly about hours of work, mistreatment, and punishment. Their friends reiterated again and again that apprenticeship was only a modified slavery. About the only modification visible in most instances was the removal of the whip, legally at least, from the hands of the overseer—though that did not put an end to flogging. The special magistrates intervened to order flogging done in the workhouses, which was often done with excesses of brutality and bloodiness that were shocking even in a time when corporal punishment was still widely used. A series of books exposing such atrocities appeared in 1837, arousing special horror over the flogging and torture of women on treadmills. British humanitarians convinced people at home that they had been cheated and swindled into paying compensation for slaves who continued under a more brutal slavery. As a training for freedom, apprenticeship had consigned the freedman to compulsory labor that provided no experience of freedom. Returning to the battle, English abolitionists and humanitarians marshaled their forces to put an end to apprenticeship and declare full freedom, which was done in 1838.[14]

Getting wind of Parliament's intentions, the assemblies of the self-governing colonies anticipated the move by abolishing the apprenticeship system themselves as of August 1, 1838, rather than acknowledge British dictation. They accompanied this act with stiff and sullen assertions of their right of self-government, "confirmed by time, usage, and law," in matters of taxation, police laws, and local affairs. Their purpose was to retain control over black labor and in effect subvert the humanitarian revolution of civil rights the home government sought to impose. The English Radicals rebelled, but the newly crowned queen intervened, and the government bowed to the defiant colonial assemblies. The Radicals and humanitarians got their abolition law and civil rights laws, but the local control remained in the hands of the small ruling class of masters, who had ruled under slavery.

William R. Brock, an English historian, has suggested in a book on Reconstruction that one root of America's trouble in enforcing the law in the South lay in the national commitment to an outmoded eighteenth-century Constitution with archaic checks and balances, states' rights, and other inhibitions on majority rule and national authority. These restraints, he points out, shielded the southern states from Radical reform and encouraged them to resist northern terms. In his opinion, "a drastic solution imposed by a simple majority unhampered by checks and balances"—in other words, a proper English parliamentary procedure—would have prevented failure.[15] Perhaps. But Britain's own experience with enforcing Radical parliamentary rule in the West Indies does not strengthen this argument. Parliament, like Congress, was faced with a states' rights and home rule crisis, and the Radicals of Parliament gave in quicker than the Radicals of Congress. In effect, Jamaica got home rule before being subjected to radical reconstruction, instead of afterward as was the case of most southern states. The Jamaicans and Barbadians won their struggle in the short run more completely than the Alabamians and Louisianians won theirs, but did not retain the fruits of victory so long.

Monopoly of political power enabled masters to extend their control over labor by legislation. Coercive purposes were concealed in "innocent looking" enactments, such as a police act prohibiting persons from transporting produce without written permission from the owner of the land, which could easily be used to prevent illiterate settlers from marketing their crops. Other laws were more forthright in purpose. Stringent vagrancy acts permitted "anyone," that is, any white person or his agent, in the absence of police to arrest a vagrant; another law made workmen liable to three months' imprisonment with hard labor "for any misconduct whatever." The special magistrates used under apprenticeship were retained, and a new law declared that their "authority over the manual laborers of Jamaica will be peremptory and unlimited in the highest degree."[16]

The failure of these efforts at full labor control in some islands, such as Jamaica and especially Trinidad and Guiana, was associated with two interrelated conditions: the decline in production and prosperity of the sugar plantations and an abundance of uncultivated land. The first demand of emancipated slaves was always for land. It was so among those of the southern states in 1865, but there the solution more nearly approximated that of Antigua, Barbados, and the Lesser Antilles. In islands with no extra land, the freedmen had little choice but to return to work for the white man. There was extra land in the South, but that which was most available was quickly snatched from their grasp by the frustration of the Freedmen's Bureau plans for distributing abandoned lands, and the less available land was beyond their reach for lack of capital.[17] In Jamaica little more than a third of the arable land was under cultivation at the time of emancipation, and the number of uncultivated acres was annually increased by bankruptcies and the abandonment of plantations. Freedmen could not be kept off these lands, either by law or private agreement. Over the years a substantial independent black peasantry of small landholders developed. The same thing occurred in Trinidad and British Guiana, where even more land was available. All these movements diminished planter control over the blacks.[18]

In colonies where this occurred, planters regularly resorted to large-scale importations of contract coolie labor from the Orient. The history of coolie labor comes near to matching the history of slavery in human exploitation, misery, and degradation. Often transported farther from their native land than the Africans had been and in much the same manner, the Orientals were dumped in environments often more hostile to them than to Africans and without such minimal protection as was afforded by a owner with an investment to safeguard or missionaries with consciences to serve. They were sometimes advertised, sold, and treated like cattle. Slavery had given way to forced labor under a new guise, with different races under the yoke. Before the British stopped the immigration of contract labor in 1917, Guiana imported 239,000 East Indians and 14,000 Chinese, and Trinidad took in 135,000 East Indians. Other colonies made smaller imports. The

French imported about 65,000 East Indians for their Caribbean colonies, and the Dutch took in at their colony of Surinam 34,848 East Indians and 30,905 Javanese over a long period.[19]

Nothing in the southern experience compares with the coolie labor solution. It is not that southern planters were indifferent to Caribbean experiments with coolies. They were extremely interested. They were as sure as their West Indian counterparts that freedmen would not work the plantation without compulsion, and they sought substitutes. They organized companies, held conventions, even sent an agent to China to promote coolie imports, but the federal government frowned on the idea, the planters lacked capital, and only a handful of coolies actually turned up in Dixie.[20] This made a great deal of difference in the distinctive adjustment the South made to free labor. The Dutch, for example, imported twice as many East Indians and Javanese as they emancipated Africans in Surinam, and between them Trinidad and Guiana imported as many coolies as the United States imported African slaves in its whole history. The Mauritian planters, as one historian puts it, solved "the industrial problem of emancipation . . . by the elimination of the negroes" and were thus able "to escape from the task of converting slaves into free laborers."[21] This escape from the basic problem of emancipation and readjustment was only partially available to planters in the Caribbean and not at all to planters in the American South.

Cuban planters anticipated the abolition of slavery by four decades in their use of coolie labor both as a supplement to and a substitute for slave labor. Beginning in 1847 great numbers of Chinese coolies were imported, sold, bought, transferred, and worked in the manner of slaves, though nominally they were "voluntarily obligated" by eight-year contracts. Official regulations of 1849 authorized the use of whips, irons, and imprisonment for coolies who resisted labor or disobeyed orders. They died in great numbers and suicides were frequent, yet over the next quarter of a century more than 124,000 coolies reached Cuba. These were also years of the heaviest imports of African slaves.[22]

The new masters of postabolition Brazil, with a coffee boom and an industrial expansion on their hands, had taken drastic measures to anticipate the shortage of labor. Using state subsidies, they recruited nearly a million European immigrants, most of them on a contract-labor basis, in the 1880s and 1890s. Coffee planters and industrialists drove their immigrant labor, the majority of them Italian peasants, as ruthlessly as they had driven slaves until a renewed labor shortage forced them to relent.[23]

Much has been made of benevolent Iberian slavery and race relations during slavery as a superior preparation for freedom. Whatever restraint Spain had exerted over Cuban labor policy to protect the blacks came to an end twelve years after abolition, when Cuba won its independence. In effect Cuba won home rule, not so quickly as Jamaica but at precisely the interval after abolition as South Carolina and Louisiana. Home rule in Cuba meant much the same as home rule in Jamaica and Mississippi: the rule of the whites and the exclusion of the blacks. At least the two dominant political parties of independent Cuba proclaimed that to be their purpose. Both came out squarely for white supremacy and agreed that Negroes "constitute a depraved and inferior race which must be kept in its proper place in a white man's society."[24]

Brazilians are especially noted for their claims of racial felicity and patriarchal benevolence. One Brazilian historian maintains that "there was nothing [in Brazil] which can be compared with the period of Reconstruction in the United States." Certainly there were differences, but anyone acquainted with Reconstruction in the South will find in postabolition Brazil much that is comparable. The familiar "mass exodus from the plantations" occurred on schedule. There were the standard days of jubilation and the usual pictures of former slaves "wandering in groups along the roads with no destination," changing plantations, seeking lost relatives and of the old and decrepit, to whom freedom "brought hunger and death" and abandonment by their masters. In the early days the freedmen appeared "disoriented, not knowing what to do with their freedom," many of them "dazed by the rapidity of the transformation." Where possible, planters clung to the old plantation routine. A rumor spread among freedmen that a small plot of land was to be granted each former slave, but nothing came of it. Like southern planters, Brazilians complained that freedmen confused freedom with laziness. Like them too, Brazilian planters avoided creating a black peasantry by refusing to sell them land. Like southerners, they tried the wage system, gave it up, and turned their labor force into sharecroppers under the lien system while planters became supply merchants—the Brazilian-southern escape by compromise from the classic problem of "converting slaves into free laborers."[25] Few know what went on in the backcountry, the depressed sugar country of the northeast, Brazil's counterpart of the American South. A modern writer asks whether slaves there were "really emancipated or merely freed from the name of slave? The fact is that whether he was slave or serf, farmhand, sharecropper or leaseholder, the Brazilian peasant, at least in the Northeast, has always been accustomed to forced labor, hunger, and misery."[26] The long legacy of slavery was much the same here as elsewhere.

There is no space here for comparative analysis of the political adjustment to freedom, but it would be more a study of contrast than comparison. For nowhere in plantation America during the nineteenth century did the white man share with black freedmen the range of political power and office that the southern whites were forced to share briefly with their freedmen. Not even in the British West Indies, with their overwhelming preponderance of blacks, was there anything that could be described as "Black Reconstruction." In effect the blacks, though nominally emancipated, were quickly eliminated from politics. It is true that a class of "browns" or "coloreds" did gain a share of office and political power, but that is another story.[27]

This introduces the infinitely complicated subject of comparative race relations. To do it justice would require a whole book, but some notice of it is essential and I shall have to oversimplify. In general, I believe race prejudice and discrimination were universal in plantation America. I find very helpful a distinction that a Brazilian scholar, Oracy Nogueira, has drawn between two models of prejudice, "prejudice of mark" and "prejudice of origin." The latter type, prejudice of origin, in its pure form is peculiar to the United States. It is directed at anyone, regardless of physical appearance or personal attribute, known to be in any degree of African origin. This peculiar white myth of what constitutes a "black" is so universal in the United States as to be accepted by so-called black nationalists. Elsewhere, particularly in Latin America, prejudice varies according to "mark," physical or otherwise, and discriminates fastidiously among all the infinite varieties, as well as personal attributes and attainments, that amalgamations between Africans and other races can produce. In that sense, prejudice of mark is literally more discriminating than prejudice of origin, though the pure black appears to suffer as much exclusion from the one as from the other type.[28]

The British West Indies fall somewhere between the two models in their recognition of a separate caste of "coloreds" or "browns" between whites and blacks, sharing some of the privileges of the former and some of the penalties of the latter. During the thirty years after abolition, whites and blacks drifted farther and farther apart into separate cultures, economies, and religions. The coloreds were no help in mediating between races, for their relations with blacks were worse than those between whites and blacks. The browns renounced their black heritage and identified with the whites. The early 1860s were a time of social tension, economic depression, and natural disasters in Jamaica. The contrast between their former glory and wealth and their current poverty and misery sent whites in search of scapegoats. In this search white Jamaicans anticipated the whole demonology of Reconstruction among southern whites, with their own varieties of carpetbagger, scalawag, missionary, Radical, Freedmen's Bureau, and most of all the Negro—the lazy good-for-nothing Quashee of the classic stereotype, to which Thomas Carlyle lent his famous name. The old paternalistic ambivalence of slavery days toward blacks, half genial, half contemptuous, gave way to feelings of insecurity, fear, and withdrawal. One source of this was a steady decline in the number of whites, both absolutely and relatively. By 1861 whites had dropped to 14,000 out of 441,000, only 3.1 percent, and the blacks were rapidly increasing. "In Jamaica," writes Philip Curtin, "the race question was often hidden behind other issues, while in the American South other issues tended to hide behind racial conflict." The blacks of Jamaica seemed stronger and more suspicious in the mid-sixties. A weird religious revival seized them, mixed with economic discontent and protest.[29]

There had been other local riots, bloodshed, and lootings since abolition, but the Morant Bay riot of October, 1865, came in a time of great distress and social tension. It sprang from no revolutionary ideology and was over in two days of sporadic violence that took the lives of 22 and left 34 wounded, some shops looted, and 5 buildings burned—nearly all confined to one parish. But a hysterical governor declared it islandwide, conspiratorial, and insurrectionary and released uninstructed soldiers and colored maroons upon the people. In all they killed 439, many with excessive brutality; flogged 600 men and women with fifty to a hundred lashes, often with cruelly wired whips; and burned 1,000 huts, cottages, and buildings, most of them belonging to the poorest blacks. And then in the ensuing panic the whites voted to abandon what they had held for thirty years essential to their very existence—home rule and self-government—and the Colonial Office, swayed by stories of Negro fiendishness, approved the end of representative government and took over from the frightened planters.[30]

Southerners were destined to repeat many of the errors of Jamaica, but not in their wildest excesses, not even those of New Orleans and Memphis in 1866, did they come near approximating the bloodbath of Morant Bay. The garbled and exaggerated account of the Jamaican tragedy that southern whites read in their newspapers opened an appalling vision of the future. In October, 1865, the whites of the crushed and defeated Confederacy faced with anxiety most of the uncertainties and terrors of their own ordeal of free labor and Negro equality. Would freedmen work without compulsion? Were they prepared for freedom and self-government? Was race war inevitable? For thirty years they had debated with American abolitionists the success of emancipation in the West Indies. The abolitionists felt they had the better of the old argument. But the news from Jamaica in the fall of 1865 seemed to southerners the final word in the old debate, the confirmation of their views: freedom was a failure in the West Indies.[31]

And so it was, in a manner of speaking. And so would the southerners' own more gigantic experiment with freedom fail. And they might have gone further and pointed out its failure throughout plantation America. But failure, like most human experience, is relative. It depends on expectations and promises, on commitments and capabilities. One man's failure is another man's success. And in a way the American failure was the greatest of all. For in 1865 the democratic colossus of the New World stood triumphant, flushed with the terrible victories at Gettysburg, Vicksburg, and Appomattox. Its crusade for freedom had vindicated the blood shed by its sons, and in the full flush of power and victory and righteousness its leaders solemnly pledged the nation to fulfill its promises, not only of freedom but also the full measure of democracy and racial equality. The powers of fulfillment, sealed by the sacrifices of a victorious war, were seemingly unlimited, though of course they were not. At least the federal government was no remote transatlantic metropolitan parliament on the banks of the Thames or the Seine. It sat on the Potomac, with General Robert E. Lee's Arlington mansion in full view of the White House windows across the river, and its armies garrisoned the defeated states.

Yet we know that, although the North won its four-year war against a fully armed, mobilized, and determined South when the issue was slavery, it very quickly lost its crusade against a disarmed, defeated, and impoverished South when the issue was equality. For on this issue the South was united as it had not been on slavery. And the North was even more divided on the issue of equality than it had been on slavery. In fact, when the chips were down, the overwhelmingly preponderant views of the North on that issue were in no important respect different from those of the South—and never had been.

Notes

Notes to JUBILEE AND BEYOND: WHAT WAS FREEDOM?
by Willie Lee Rose

1. Allan Nevins, *The War for the Union: War Becomes Revolution, 1862–1863* (New York, 1960); David Brion Davis, "Abolitionists and the Freed-men: An Essay Review," *Journal of Southern History,* XXXI (May 1965), 189; C. Vann Woodward, *The Burden of Southern History* (Rev. ed.; Baton Rouge, 1968), 70; Willie Lee Rose, *Rehearsal for Reconstruction* (Indianapolis, 1964).

2. C. Vann Woodward, "White Racism and Black Emancipation," *New York Review of Books,* February 27, 1969, p. 8; Jacques Voegeli, *Free But Not Equal: The Midwest and the Negro During the Civil War* (Chicago, 1968); Richard O. Curry, "The Abolitionists and Reconstruction: A Critical Appraisal," *Journal of Southern History,* XXXIV (November–December, 1968); Forrest G. Wood, *Black Score: The Racist Response to Emancipation and Reconstruction* (Berkeley, 1969); William S. McFeely, *Yankee Stepfather: General O. O. Howard and the Freedmen* (New Haven, 1968).

3. This is the standard view, and the frequent appearance of these phrases obviates the need for specific citations.

4. Louis S. Gerteis, *From Contraband to Freedman: Federal Policy Toward Blacks, 1861–65* (Westport, Conn., 1973), 3, 5.

5. W. Logan Razford, *The Negro in American Life and Thought: The Nadir, 1877–1901* (New York, 1954); C. Vann Woodward, *Origins of the New South, 1877–1913* (Baton Rouge, 1951).

6. This, of course, is the interpretation of the Fourteenth Amendment given in the famous *Slaughterhouse* decision of 1873. The *Civil Rights Cases* of 1883 held that the Fourteenth Amendment prohibited invasion of civil rights of individuals by the state governments, but that it could not protect individuals who were denied their civil rights by other individuals. This protection was left to state action.

7. C. Vann Woodward, *Reunion and Reaction: The Compromise of 1877 and the End of Reconstruction* (Boston, 1951).

8. William Cohen, "Negro Involuntary Servitude in the South, 1865–1940: A Preliminary Analysis," *Journal of Southern History*, XLII (February, 1976), 31–60; Pete Daniel, *The Shadow of Slavery: Peonage in the South, 1901–1969* (Urbana, 1972); Theodore Brantner Wilson, *The Black Codes of the South* (University, Ala., 1965).

9. For examples, see Joel Williamson, *After Slavery* (Chapel Hill, 1965), 50–53, 258–66; Gerteis, *From Contraband to Freedman*, 107–15; Rose, *Rehearsal for Reconstruction*, 107–109; Wood, *Black Score*, 140–43; Otis A. Singletary, *The Black Militia* (Austin, 1957).

10. Willie Lee Rose, "Masters Without Slaves" (Paper delivered at the American Historical Association annual meeting, 1965).

11. Gerteis, *From Contraband to Freedman*, 111–15.

12. Rose, *Rehearsal for Reconstruction*, esp. Ch. 5, 7, and 10.

13. Edwin D. Hoffman, "From Slavery to Self-Reliance," *Journal of Negro History*, XLI (January, 1956), 8–42.

14. Most authors have concluded that the Southern Homestead Act of 1866, rescinded in 1876, was not effective so far as blacks were concerned.

15. Woodward, "White Racism and Black Emancipation."

16. One of the points stressed by Robert W. Fogel and Stanley L. Engerman in *Time on the Cross* (2 vols.; Boston, 1975) to support their thesis on the profitability of plantation labor was that the large farms benefited from advantages of scale. It is true that rice never recovered in the low country of South Carolina and Georgia after the war and that the area was the scene of the largest disruption in land tenure.

17. James T. Currie, "Vicksburg, 1863–1870: The Promise and the Reality of Reconstruction on the Mississippi" (Ph.D. dissertation, University of Virginia, 1975).

18. Rose, *Rehearsal for Reconstruction*. By 1960 the freeholds on St. Helena Island, where land had been confiscated and divided among slaves at favorable prices, were subdivided as Philbrick had suggested they would be.

19. Gerteis, *From Contraband to Freedman*, Ch. 6, esp. 106–15.

20. In this I follow the reasoning of Eric McKitrick, *Andrew Johnson and Reconstruction* (Chicago, 1965).

21. Charles B. Dew, "Disciplining Slave Ironworkers in the Antebellum South: Coercion, Conciliation, and Accommodation," *American Historical Review*, LXXIX (April, 1974), 393.

22. Ira Berlin, *Slaves Without Masters: The Free Negro in the Antebellum South* (New York, 1974).

23. William Channing Gannett, letter of April 28, 1865, in *Freedmen's Record*, I (June, 1865), 93.

24. Williamson, *After Slavery*, 63.

Notes to W. E. B. DU BOIS AS A HEGELIAN
by Joel Williamson

1. Du Bois first published his "Strivings" essay in the *Atlantic Monthly* in 1897 under the title "Strivings of the Negro People." With only minor revisions, he republished it in 1903 in *The Souls of Black Folk* as the lead

and theme-setting essay. W. E. B. Du Bois, "Strivings of the Negro People," *Atlantic Monthly*, LXXX (July, 1897), 194–98; W. E. B. Du Bois, *The Souls of Black Folk: Essays and Sketches* (3rd ed.; Chicago, 1903), 1–12. The quotations that follow from the "Strivings" essay are taken from the latter source.

2. Georg Wilhelm Friedrich Hegel, *The Philosophy of History* (New York, 1956), 98.

3. *Ibid.*, 80.

4. Francis L. Broderick, *W. E. B. Du Bois: Negro Leader in a Time of Crisis* (Stanford, 1959), 21.

5. Hegel, *The Philosophy of History*, 1–79 *passim*. The quotation is taken from p. 19.

6. *Ibid.*, 341ff.

7. *Ibid.*, 103–10, 112–15.

8. Du Bois, *The Souls of Black Folk*, 3. In voodoo belief, the seventh son is the fortunate one, and to be born with a veil is to have the gift of prophesy.

9. Hegel, *The Philosophy of History*, 86–87.

10. Du Bois, *The Souls of Black Folk*, 5–8.

11. *Ibid.*, 2.

12. W. E. B. Du Bois, *The Autobiography of W. E. B. Du Bois: A Soliloquy on Viewing My Life from the Last Decade of Its First Century* (New York, 1968), 105 108, 113–20, 132.

13. *Ibid.*, 133.

14. Samuel E. Morrison (ed.), *The Development of Harvard University, Since the Inauguration of President Eliot, 1869–1929* (Cambridge, Mass., 1930), 20; Ralph Barton Perry, *The Thought and Character of William James* (New York, 1954), 161.

15. Du Bois, *Autobiography*, 113.

16. Perry, *William James*, 161–62.

17. George Santayana, *Persons and Places: The Background of My Life* (New York, 1944), I, 241.

18. Du Bois, *Autobiography*, 143.

19. Morrison (ed.), *Harvard University*, 319.

20. For Shaler's thought, see Nathaniel Southgate Shaler, "The Negro Problem," *Atlantic Monthly*, LIV (November, 1884), 696–709; *idem*, "Science and the African Problem," *Atlantic Monthly*, LXVI (July, 1890), 36–45; *idem*, *The Neighbor: The Natural History of Human Contacts* (Boston and New York, 1904).

21. Du Bois, *Autobiography*, 143.

22. Broderick, *Du Bois*, 15–17.

23. Du Bois, *Autobiography*, 146.

24. *Ibid.*, 148.

25. *Ibid.*

26. Broderick, *Du Bois*, 26–27.

27. Du Bois, *Autobiography*, 164.

28. Broderick, *Du Bois*, 28–29. See also Du Bois, *Autobiography*, 170–71.

29. Du Bois, *Autobiography*, 126.

30. Hegel, *The Philosophy of History*, 29–31.

31. Broderick, *Du Bois*, 18–20.
32. *Ibid.*, 227.
33. *Ibid.*, 128.

Notes to SHARECROPPING: MARKET RESPONSE OR MECHANISM OF RACE CONTROL?
by Richard Sutch and Roger Ransom

1. Alfred Conrad and John Meyer, "The Economics of Slavery in the Ante Bellum South," *Journal of Political Economy*, LXVI (April, 1958).
2. Hugh G. Aitken (ed.), *Did Slavery Pay?* (Boston, 1971).
3. A major part of this work is presented in William N. Parker (ed.), *The Structure of the Cotton Economy of the Antebellum South* (Washington, D.C., 1970).
4. Robert W. Fogel and Stanley L. Engerman, *Time on the Cross* (2 vols.; Boston, 1974).
5. A book-length critique of the Fogel-Engerman thesis can be found in Paul A. David *et al.*, *Reckoning with Slavery: A Critical Study in the Quantitative History of American Negro Slavery* (New York, 1976). For a sampling of historians' current perspectives on the problems posed by American slavery, see Harry P. Owens (ed.), *Perspectives and Irony in American Slavery* (Jackson, Miss., 1976).
6. Economists have not been studying the Reconstruction South very long, and the firstfruits of this work have only recently appeared. Our own work on the South began in 1968 when we organized the Southern Economic History Project at the University of California. The major results of that study appear in Roger Ransom and Richard Sutch, *One Kind of Freedom: The Economic Consequences of Emancipation* (New York, 1977). Two other economists have published studies of the South after the Civil War: Stephen DeCanio, *Agriculture in the Postbellum South: The Economics of Production and Supply* (Cambridge, Mass., 1974); and Robert Higgs, *Competition and Coercion: Blacks in the American Economy* (New York, 1977).
7. Kenneth M. Stampp, *The Peculiar Institution: Slavery in the Antebellum South* (New York, 1956), 42.
8. See Ransom and Sutch, *One Kind of Freedom*, 68.
9. F. W. Loring and C. F. Atkinson, *Cotton Culture and the South Considered with Reference to Emigration* (Boston, 1869), 33.
10. Robert Somers, *The Southern States Since the War, 1870–1* (New York, 1871), 128.
11. See Ransom and Sutch, *One Kind of Freedom*, Ch. 5. Examples of such observations can be found in Whitelaw Reid, *After the War: A Tour of the Southern States, 1865–1866* (New York, 1965), 572, first published in 1866; and John T. Trowbridge, *The Desolate South, 1865–1866* (Boston, 1956), 195, 214, originally published in 1866 as *The South, a Journey Through the Desolated States*.
12. That compulsion was largely responsible for the efficiency of gang labor in the antebellum South is widely acknowledged by students of the

slave system. Fogel and Engerman, who undertook one of the most detailed examinations of the sources of efficiency in the slave system, emphasize material reward, but agree with other scholars that coercion was the crucial factor in making the work gang productive. See Fogel and Engerman, *Time on the Cross*, I, 237. See also Herbert G. Gutman and Richard Sutch, "Sambo Makes Good; or, Were Slaves Imbued with the Protestant Work Ethic?" in David *et al.*, *Reckoning with Slavery*.

13. Based on a sample of plantations in 1859, we estimate that the average value of the product of a slave's labor was $62.46 and the value of consumption articles (food, clothing, etc.) provided the slave was only $28.95. This suggests that the master expropriated 53.7 percent of the slave's labor product. On plantations with fifty-one or more slaves our estimate of the rate of exploitation was 59.2 percent. See Ransom and Sutch, *One Kind of Freedom*, Ch. 1, Table 1.1, p. 3, for a more complete discussion of these calculations of the rate of exploitation.

14. Our estimate is based on a comparison of labor participation of blacks under slavery in the late 1850s and their participation as free workers in the 1870s. See *ibid.*, App. C, for a full explanation of the procedure used to estimate the withdrawal of labor.

15. Loring and Atkinson, *Cotton Culture*, 109–10.

16. Acreage data for 1860 and 1870 are summarized in U.S. Census Office, Tenth Census, *Report on the Production of Agriculture, June 1, 1880* (Washington, D.C., 1883), III, 11, 16. These figures provide only a rough guide to the actual fall in acreage, inasmuch as the 1870 enumeration in the South was unquestionably less complete than in 1860.

17. Ransom and Sutch, *One Kind of Freedom*, 9.

18. We also point out that the fall in per capita output cannot be attributed to the destructive impact of the Civil War. The loss of capital and workstock that occurred during that war went largely unnoticed after the war because of the much larger decline in the labor available to work with it. Had there been no destruction of capital or animals during the war, the South, with a reduced supply of labor, would still have been unable to restore the output to prewar levels. For a fuller discussion of this point, see Roger Ransom and Richard Sutch, "The Impact of the Civil War and of Emancipation on Southern Agriculture," *Explorations in Economic History*, XII (January, 1975).

19. Sidney Andrews, *The South Since the War, as Shown by Fourteen Weeks of Travel and Observation in Georgia and the Carolinas* (New York, 1970), 206, 220, first published in 1866.

20. Trowbridge, *The Desolate South*, 196.

21. Loring and Atkinson, *Cotton Culture*, 32.

22. D. Wyatt Aiken, "Does Farming Pay in the South?" *Rural Carolinian*, II (March, 1871), 324.

23. Trowbridge, *The Desolate South*, 194.

24. Andrews, *The South Since the War*, 206.

25. Reid, *After the War*, 564–65; U.S. Congress, *The Ku Klux Conspiracy: Report of the Joint Select Committee*, House of Representatives Report No. 22, 42nd Cong., 2nd Sess. (Washington, D.C., 1872).

26. The estimated return per laborer on both sharecropped and rented farms was about $60, based on our 1880 sample of farms. The total labor return to family tenant farms in that year was just under $200. See Ransom and Sutch, *One Kind of Freedom*, Table 5.6, p. 100 and Table A.10 p. 219.

27. A wage laborer in the South in 1880 seldom averaged much over $8 to $10 per month or between $108 and $120 per year if the man was employed throughout the year. Women and children received substantially lower rates and generally did not work full-time. See U.S. Department of Agriculture, Bureau of Statistics, *Wages of Farm Labor: Nineteenth Investigation, in 1909, Continuing a Series That Began in 1866*, USDA Bureau of Statistics Bulletin No. 99 (Washington, D.C., 1912).

28. We argue in our book that there was indeed a form of exploitation in southern agriculture at this time. Small farmers and farm laborers were victimized by rural storekeepers, who held a monopoly over credit. Their mechanism of exploitation, however, was only indirectly related to tenancy and had little to do with the terms of the sharecropping contract. See Ransom and Sutch, *One Kind of Freedom*, Ch. 6–8, and *idem*, "The 'Lockin' Mechanism and Overproduction of Cotton in the Postbellum South," *Agricultural History*, XLIX (April, 1975).

29. The estimates of per capita crop output in constant prices between 1869 and 1909 are presented in Ransom and Sutch, *One Kind of Freedom*, Table 9.12, p. 194. The gross estimates were divided by our estimate of the rural population of the South based on the census bench marks. The estimates of gross national product for the United States are from U.S. Bureau of the Census, *Historical Statistics of the United States, Colonial Times to 1957* (Washington, D.C., 1960), Ser. F-4, p. 139.

30. For a more extensive analysis of the role of annual contracting in southern sharecropping, see D. Gale Johnson, "Resource Allocation Under Share Contracts," *Journal of Political Economy*, LVIII (April, 1950), 111–23.

31. *Southern Cultivator*, XXIX (March, 1871), 90.

32. The 1880 figures are based on our sample of farms from the cotton South. See Ransom and Sutch, *One Kind of Freedom*, Table 5.1, p. 84. The figure for 1900 is for the states of South Carolina, Georgia, Alabama, Mississippi, and Louisiana and is computed from the data in U.S. Census Office, *Twelfth Census, 1900, Census Reports* (Washington, D.C., 1902), V, 158–85.

Notes to AFTER EMANCIPATION
by George M. Fredrickson

1. Frank Tannenbaum, *Slave and Citizen: The Negro in the Americas* (New York, 1946).

2. A few sociologists, however, have tried in a very general way to make interhemispheric comparisons of patterns of racial dominance and exploitation. See, for example, Wilhelmina Kloosterboer, *Involuntary Servitude Since the Abolition of Slavery: A Survey of Compulsory Labor Through-*

out the World (Leiden, 1960); Phillip Mason, *Patterns of Dominance* (London, 1970); and Pierre L. van den Berghe, *Race and Racism: A Comparative Perspective* (New York, 1967).

3. See Magnus Morner, *Race Mixture in the History of Latin America* (Boston, 1967), 67–70.

4. David Brion Davis, *The Problem of Slavery in the Age of Revolution, 1770–1823* (Ithaca, 1975).

5. For Republican ideology and attitudes toward the South, see especially Eric Foner, *Free Soil, Free Labor, Free Men: The Ideology of the Republican Party Before the Civil War* (New York, 1970).

6. See George M. Fredrickson, *The Inner Civil War: Northern Intellectuals and the Crisis of the Union* (New York, 1965), 183–216; *idem, The Black Image in the White Mind: The Debate on Afro-American Character and Destiny* (New York, 1971), 165–282 *passim*; Christine Bolt, *Victorian Attitudes to Race* (London and Toronto, 1971), 75–108, 206–18; and Richard Hofstadter, *Social Darwinism in American Thought* (Rev. ed.; Boston, 1955).

7. The literature on these developments is vast, but see especially C. Vann Woodward, *The Strange Career of Jim Crow* (3rd rev. ed.; New York, 1974); and J. Morgan Kousser, *The Shaping of Southern Politics: Suffrage Restriction and the Establishment of a One-Party South, 1880–1910* (New Haven and London, 1974).

8. See Philip D. Curtin, *The Two Jamaicas: The Role of Ideas in a Tropical Colony, 1830–1865* (Cambridge, Mass., 1955); and Douglas Hall, *Free Jamaica, 1838–1865: An Economic History* (New Haven, 1959).

9. Bolt, *Victorian Attitudes*, 90ff.

10. See C. F. J. Muller, *Die Britse Owerheid en Die Groot Trek* (Cape Town and Johannesburg, 1948); W. H. Macmillan, *The Cape Colour Question* (London, 1927); Eric A. Walker, *The Great Trek* (4th ed.; London, 1960); and J. A. I. Agar-Hamilton, *The Native Policy of the Voortrekkers: An Essay in the History of the Interior of South Africa, 1836–1858* (Cape Town, 1928).

11. See T. R. H. Davenport, "The Consolidation of a New Society: The Cape Colony," in Monica Wilson and Leonard Thompson (eds.), *The Oxford History of South Africa* (New York and Oxford, 1969), I, 272–333; J. L. McCracken, *The Cape Parliament, 1854–1910* (Oxford, 1967); and H. J. and R. E. Simons, *Class and Colour in South Africa, 1850–1950* (Middlesex, England, 1969), 11–33.

12. See Maurice J. Evans, *Black and White in South East Africa: A Study in Sociology* (London, 1911), for a graphic description of casual race mixing and the absence of public discrimination in Cape Town in the early years of the twentieth century. On crown colony rule in Jamaica, see Samuel J. Hurwitz and Edith E. Hurwitz, *Jamaica: A Historical Portrait* (New York, 1971), 175–92.

13. See the population table in Douglas Hall, "Jamaica," in David W. Cohen and Jack P. Greene (eds.), *Neither Slave Nor Free: The Freedmen of African Descent in the Slave Societies of the New World* (Baltimore and London, 1972), 194.

14. Quoted in Hurwitz and Hurwitz, *Jamaica*, 63.
15. Anton V. Long, *Jamaica and the New Order, 1827–1847* (Jamaica, 1956), 1.
16. Curtin, *Two Jamaicas*, 43–46, 174–77; Hall, "Jamaica," pp. 203–208.
17. Curtin, *Two Jamaicas*, 16.
18. H. P. Jacobs, *Sixty Years of Change, 1806–1866* (Jamaica, 1973), 12–13.
19. *Ibid.*, 14.
20. On the economic consequences of emancipation in Jamaica, see especially Hall, *Free Jamaica*.
21. For a good summary of economic and social conditions in the Cape up to the 1830s, see C. W. de Kiewiet, *A History of South Africa: Social and Economic* (London, 1941), 2–55.
22. Macmillan, *The Cape Colour Question*, 141. The nonnegroid aborigines, called Hottentots by the Europeans, are now more properly denoted by anthropologists and historians as Khoi or Khoi-Khoi. The term Hottentot is currently used in South Africa as a derogatory epithet for Cape Coloreds. But to avoid confusion I have retained the usage of the white historical sources. No disparagement is intended, and quotation marks, though not used, are implied.
23. M. F. Katzen, "White Settlers and the Origin of a New Society," in Wilson and Thompson (eds.), *Oxford History*, I, 204–206. A somewhat unsatisfactory general account of South African slavery is in Victor de Kock, *Those in Bondage* (Pretoria, 1963).
24. See J. H. Marais, *The Cape Coloured People, 1652–1937* (London, 1939), 1–31; Richard Elphick, "The Cape Khoi and the First Phase of Southern Race Relations" (Ph.D. dissertation, Yale University, 1972); and P. J. van der Merwe, *Die Trekboer in die Geskiedenis van die Kaap Kolonie* (Cape Town, 1938).
25. An apparently reliable description of early race mixture at the Cape by an anonymous South African historian of this locally sensitive subject is "Miscegenation at the Cape during the Dutch East India Company's Regime, 1652–1795," *Race Relations Journal*, XX, No. 2 (1953), 23–27. Convincing evidence that offspring of interracial unions were often assimilated into the European community can be found in a recent work by an Afrikaner genealogist tracing the remote ancestry of present-day Afrikaner families. See J. A. Hesse, *Die Herkoms van die Afrikaner* (Cape Town, 1971). See also Sheila Patterson, "Some Speculations on the Status and Role of the Free People of Colour in the Western Cape," in Meyer Fortes and Sheila Patterson (eds.), *Studies in African Social Anthropology* (London, 1975), 176–78. This early tendency toward intermarriage and assimilation seems to have been encouraged for a time by the Dutch East India Company, which had a tradition of promoting certain kinds of race mixture in its eastern possessions, out of a belief that half-castes made loyal and dependable colonists and company servants. The most notable early governor of the Cape Colony, Simon van der Stel, was himself of mixed white and East Indian parentage and would be classified as colored in contemporary South Africa.

26. I. D. MacCrone, *Race Attitudes in South Africa: Historical, Experimental, and Psychological Studies* (London, 1957), 131–36.

27. See George Findlay, *Miscegenation* (Pretoria, 1936); and Graham Watson, *Passing for White: A Study of Racial Assimilation in a South African School* (London, 1970).

28. Davenport, "The Consolidation of a New Society," 293.

29. Muller, *Groot Trek*, 66–71; Macmillan, *The Cape Colour Question*, 233–46.

30. Kenneth M. Stampp, *The Peculiar Institution: Slavery in the Ante-Bellum South* (New York, 1956), 29–31.

31. See the table in Ira Berlin, *Slaves Without Masters: The Free Negro in the Antebellum South* (New York, 1974), 396–99.

32. See *ibid.*, 213–16, for a discussion of the de facto three-caste system in the port cities of the lower South.

33. For the importance of these variables in comparisons of race patterns in the United States and Latin America, see Carl N. Degler, *Neither Black Nor White: Slavery and Race Relations in Brazil and the United States* (New York, 1971), 40–47, 207–64; Marvin Harris, *Patterns of Race in the Americas* (New York, 1964), 79–94; and H. Hoetink, *Slavery and Race Relations in the Americas: Comparative Notes on Their Nature and Nexus* (New York, 1973), 14–20.

34. The various methods of coercive labor control that developed in the postemancipation South are well described in William Cohen, "Negro Involuntary Servitude in the South, 1865–1940: A Preliminary Analysis," *Journal of Southern History*, XLII (February, 1976), 3–30. For the role of terrorism and intimidation in denying blacks access to land, see Allen W. Trelease, *White Terror: The Ku Klux Klan Conspiracy and Southern Reconstruction* (New York, 1971), xvii, xxii, xlvii *passim*.

35. Curtin, *Two Jamaicas*, 43; Macmillan, *The Cape Colour Question*, 211–32; Marais, *Cape Coloured People*, 155–78.

36. Joseph Lowell Ragatz, *The Fall of the Planter Class in the British Caribbean, 1763–1833* (Washington, D.C., 1928), 417, 419, 443–46; Curtin, *Two Jamaicas*, 87–88.

37. Isobel Edwards, *Towards Emancipation: A Study in South African Slavery* (Cardiff, 1942), 120, 165–66.

38. *Ibid.*, 177–79, 187; W. L. Burn, *Emancipation and Apprenticeship in the British West Indies* (London, 1937).

39. Edwards, *Towards Emancipation*, 197–204; Muller, *Groot Trek*, 50–80; Walker, *The Great Trek*.

40. Curtin, *Two Jamaicas*, 74, 174–84; Hurwitz and Hurwitz, *Jamaica*, 143–44.

41. Curtin, *Two Jamaicas*, 182–84. See also Jacobs, *Sixty Years of Change*, 85, 87, 105, for the remarkable career of the mulatto leader Edward Jordan, who, besides being an assemblyman, served on the three-member Executive Committee of the Assembly, as mayor of Kingston, and as receiver general of the colony.

42. Long, *Jamaica and the New Order*, 90.

43. Curtin, *Two Jamaicas*, 186.

44. *Ibid.*, 184.

45. *Ibid.*, 178–203; Hall, *Free Jamaica*, 250–64. In the reign of terror unleashed by the governor after the initial disorders had subsided, 439 blacks were killed.

46. McCracken, *The Cape Parliament*, 62–70; Stanley Trapido, "White Conflict and Non-White Participation in the Politics of the Cape of Good Hope, 1853–1910" (Ph.D. dissertation, University of London, 1969), 14, 96; Phyllis Lewsen, "The Cape Liberal Tradition—Myth or Reality?" in *Collected Seminar Papers on the Societies of Southern Africa in the Nineteenth and Twentieth Centuries* (London, 1970), I, 78.

47. Trapido, "White Conflict," 110–94; McCracken, *The Cape Parliament*, 71–104; T. R. H. Davenport, *The Afrikaner Bond: The History of a South African Political Party, 1880–1911* (Cape Town, 1966), 118–23; Lewsen, "The Cape Liberal Tradition"; Leonard M. Thompson, *The Unification of South Africa, 1902–1910* (Oxford, 1960).

48. Black suffrage caused grave misgivings even within the ranks of die-hard British abolitionists and humanitarians concerned with the fate of the American freedmen. See Christine Bolt, *The Anti-Slavery Movement and Reconstruction: A Study in Anglo-American Cooperation, 1833–1877* (London, 1969), 163–69.

49. Fredrickson, *Black Image*, 58–70.

50. Jacobs, *Sixty Years of Change*, 64–65.

51. See Fredrickson, *Black Image*, 198–227, for a discussion of abortive attempts to stress class rather than race as the governing principle of southern society in the period after Reconstruction.

Notes to THE PRICE OF FREEDOM
by C. Vann Woodward

1. Charles Wagley, "Plantation-America: A Culture Sphere," *Caribbean Studies*, IV (1964), 12.

2. Herbert S. Klein, *Slavery in the Americas: A Comparative Study of Virginia and Cuba* (Chicago, 1917), 123, 202; Arthur F. Corwin, *Spain and the Abolition of Slavery in Cuba, 1817–1886* (Austin and London, 1967), 146.

3. Stanley Stein, *Vassouras: A Brazilian Coffee Country, 1850–1900* (Cambridge, Mass., 1957), 294.

4. James G. Leyburn, *The Haitian People* (New Haven, 1941), 20–93; C. L. R. James, *The Black Jacobins* (New York, 1963).

5. Philip D. Curtin, *The Atlantic Slave Trade: A Census* (Madison, Wis., 1969), 88–89, Table 24.

6. Haiti, for example, imported 864,000, 9 percent of the total, or more than twice as many slaves as the whole United States. Jamaica imported 748,000, nearly twice America's total, and held only 311,070 in 1834. The tiny island of Barbados took in 387,000 or 4 percent of the total, against 4.5 percent for the continental United States. The French colonies of Martinique and Guadaloupe received 657,000 or 6.8 percent, and Cuba imported 702,000 or 7.3 percent. *Ibid.*

7. *Ibid.*, 40, Table 9 B; 46, Table 11; 268, Table 77.

8. Alexis de Tocqueville, *Report Made to the Chamber of Deputies on the Abolition of Slavery in the French Colonies* (Boston, 1841), 9–10, 16, 26–27, 46–50; Seymour Druscher (ed.), *Tocqueville and Beaumont on Social Reform* (New York, 1968), 98–173.

9. Wilhelmina Kloosterboer, *Involuntary Servitude Since the Abolition of Slavery: A Survey of Compulsory Labour Throughout the World* (Leiden, 1960), 191–203.

10. Theodore B. Wilson, *The Black Codes of the South* (University, Ala., 1965).

11. W. L. Burn, *Emancipation and Apprenticeship in the British West Indies* (London, 1937), 176–79.

12. *Ibid.*, 166n–67n.

13. Paul Knaplund, *James Stephens and the British Colonial System, 1813–1847* (Madison, Wis., 1953), 107–16; W. L. Mathieson, *British Slave Emancipation, 1838–1849* (London, 1932), 60–61, 73.

14. Burn, *Emancipation and Apprenticeship*, 340–57, 364–71; Philip D. Curtin, *The Two Jamaicas: The Role of Ideas in a Tropical Colony, 1830–1865* (Cambridge, Mass., 1955), 94–95; W. L. Mathieson, *British Slavery and its Abolition, 1823–1838* (London, 1926), 271; Mathieson, *British Slave Emancipation*, 40.

15. W. R. Brock, *An American Crisis: Congress and Reconstruction, 1865–1867* (London, 1963), 272–73.

16. Curtin, *Two Jamaicas*, 95–98; Burn, *Emancipation and Apprenticeship*, 360–61.

17. William S. McFeely, *Yankee Stepfather: General O. O. Howard and the Freedmen* (New Haven, 1968).

18. W. L. Mathieson, *The Sugar Colonies and Governor Eyre, 1849–1866* (London, 1936), 3, 72; Curtin, *Two Jamaicas*, 106–109.

19. Mathieson, *The Sugar Colonies*, 4–5, 51–52, 77; Donald Wood, *Trinidad in Transition: The Years After Slavery* (London and New York, 1968), 130–31, 136–37, 158; Leo A. Despres, *Cultural Pluralism and Nationalist Politics in British Guiana* (Chicago, 1967), 56.

20. Vernon L. Wharton, *The Negro in Mississippi, 1865–1890* (Chapel Hill, 1947), 97–103; Robert S. Henry, *The Story of Reconstruction* (New York, 1938), 364.

21. Mathieson, *British Slave Emancipation*, 130.

22. Corwin, *Spain and the Abolition of Slavery*, 109–10, 135–36.

23. Stein, *Vassouras*.

24. Philip Foner, *A History of Cuba and Its Relations with the United States* (New York, 1963), II, 293.

25. Stein, *Vassouras*, 250–72; Florestan Fernandes, *The Negro in Brazilian Society*, trans. Jacqueline D. Skiles and Burnel and Arthur Rothwell; ed. Phillis B. Evelett (New York, 1969), 1–4, 7, 14–16, 18–19, 23, 35, 42, 48, 50, 54–56, 135–37, 183.

26. Josué de Castros, *Death in the Northeast* (New York, 1966), 9.

27. H. A. Wyndham, *The Atlantic and Emancipation* (London, 1937), 120–21, 124, 130; W. G. Sewell, *The Ordeal of Free Labor in the West Indies* (New York, 1861), 37–38, 258; W. P. Livingstone, *Black Jamaica* (London, 1899), 58–61.

28. Oracy Nogueira, "Skin Color and Social Class," in *Plantation Systems of the New World* (Washington, D.C., 1959), 169.

29. Curtin, *Two Jamaicas*, 106–109, 116, 146–48, 168–77; Douglas Hall, *Free Jamaica, 1838–1865: An Economic History* (New Haven, 1959), 157–63; Lord Olivier, *The Myth of Governor Eyre* (London, 1935), 53–187; Graham Knox, "British Colonial Policy and the Problem of Establishing Free Society in Jamaica, 1838–1865," *Caribbean Studies*, II (January, 1863), 3–13.

30. Hall, *Free Jamaica*, 245–64; Livingstone, *Black Jamaica*, 58–81; Bernard Semmel, *The Governor Eyre Controversy* (London, 1962).

31. James M. McPherson, "Was West Indian Emancipation a Success? The Abolitionist Argument During the American Civil War," *Caribbean Studies*, IV (July, 1964), 28–34.